Build and Grow Your Fashion Brand

HOW TO START, SCALE, AND STAND OUT IN THE COMPETITIVE WORLD OF FASHION

Agile Fashion: Building a Brand That Adapts and Thrives in Fast-Paced Markets

PRASHANTA HV

INDIA • SINGAPORE • MALAYSIA

ISBN

Hardcase 979-8-89906-988-8
Paperback 979-8-89673-765-0

To my Mother and Father (I wish he were here), my sisters Vinutha and Savitha, my beloved wife, Neema, and my wonderful children, Sanjith and Abhinav.

Contents

Part Three: Scaling

Foreword

From factory floors to boardrooms, I've spent upwards of three and a half decades studying and shaping the fashion business in India.

It's not often that one gets the chance to witness a colleague grow into a thoughtful industry voice—one who not only lives the business but also reflects deeply on it, refines it, and chooses to share that wisdom with the next generation. HV Prashanta is one such rare individual.

I have had the privilege of working with Prashanth across two defining phases of both our careers—first at **Madura Garments (now Aditya Birla Fashions Ltd.)**, and later when I led the private label business at **Megamart (for Arvind Fashions Ltd.)**. Even back then, what stood out was his sharp mind, his relentless work ethic, and his quiet but unmistakable drive to learn. He's someone who has truly built his career from scratch, fueled not just by ambition but by a deep curiosity about how this industry works—at every level, from fabric to consumer.

Over the years, I've seen him evolve—never losing his edge, but always adding new layers of understanding. Prashant has continued to engage with fashion not just as commerce or trend, but as a living, breathing culture that reflects identity, aspiration, and innovation. This book is a natural outcome of that journey. It carries the clarity of someone who's done the hard work—not just in the field but in the mind.

"Build and Grow Your Fashion Brand" is not a book built on theory. It's a practitioner's guide—rich with frameworks, examples, and stories that only someone who has lived through the ever-changing cycles of Indian and global fashion could offer. What I particularly admire is how seamlessly it integrates high-level brand thinking with on-ground realities. Whether you're just starting up or trying to scale your brand beyond its current plateau, you'll find actionable insights at every step.

In an era where fashion is often mistaken for quick styling and faster churn, Prashant rightly brings the conversation back to **purpose**. He urges readers to ask the right questions: *Why are you starting this brand? What value do you bring to the consumer? What pain point are you solving?* These questions aren't just business tools—they are anchors. Because in fashion, trends may change, but **values**, **craft**, and **clarity of intent** are what build long-lasting legacies.

I found strong resonance between this book and my own explorations in *Fashion Fables* and *InsideApparel*. We've both seen this industry evolve—from the dominance of formalwear to the emergence of fast fashion, to now a growing wave of sustainable, purpose-driven brands. Prashant not only captures this shift with precision but also lays down a step-by-step playbook for how to thrive in it. His treatment of topics like product-market fit, brand storytelling, cultural authenticity, and MVP (Minimum Viable Product) strategy stands out for its sharpness and simplicity.

Importantly, the book doesn't just speak to fashion entrepreneurs. It speaks to **fashion entrepreneurs in India**—to those navigating the unique mix of tradition and aspiration that defines our market. It blends global best practices with local intuition, offering a nuanced approach that's hard to find in generic startup literature.

As I turned the pages, what struck me most was how personal the book feels—not just in anecdotes, but in its intent. You can tell this isn't written to impress. It's written to **serve**. To guide someone through the confusing, often overwhelming journey of building a fashion brand—from scratch, with purpose.

If you're reading this foreword, you're likely at a crossroads—either dreaming up your next venture, struggling with scale, or searching for clarity in a rapidly shifting market. Let this book be your companion. It won't just give you answers—it will help you ask better questions. And that, in the long run, is far more valuable.

To Prashant—congratulations, my friend. Your journey has always been inspiring, and with this book, you've extended that inspiration to countless others. I know how hard you've worked to get here, and I'm proud to see you now giving back with humility, insight, and heart.

Here's to more brands that are not just successful, but meaningful. And here's to the readers who will build them—better, bolder, and wiser—because they read this book.

Anindya Ray
Fashion Business Leader | Brand, Merchandising,
Design & Sourcing Strategist | Mentor
Author of *Fashion Fables* and Curator of *InsideApparel.in*

Preface

In the ever-evolving world of fashion, where trends come and go rapidly, creating a brand that stands the test of time is no small feat. It's easy to get swept up in the excitement of fleeting styles and momentary fads. Still, success lies in crafting a fashion brand anchored in purpose, sustainability, quality, and adaptability. 'Build and Grow Your Fashion Brand' offers an invaluable guide for entrepreneurs and aspiring brand founders who want to break through the noise, establish a meaningful presence, and scale their businesses sustainably.

This book is not just about creating another clothing line; it's about creating a lasting legacy in the fashion industry. From the earliest stages of developing your idea to launching your brand, to scaling it into a thriving business, this book provides the strategies and insights needed to ensure your brand not only survives but thrives in a competitive market. At the heart of this journey lies the belief that the foundation of any successful fashion brand is a strong sense of purpose. Building a brand that resonates with consumers goes beyond simply selling clothes—it's about offering products that align with their values, solve real problems, and connect with them emotionally.

'Build and Grow Your Fashion Brand' is designed to guide you through the complex process of transforming a creative vision into a profitable, long-term business. The book is divided into three parts that systematically walk you through the essential phases of building a fashion brand: nurturing your idea, positioning and launching your product, and scaling your business.

In the first part of the book, we dive deep into nurturing your brand idea. This phase is crucial because the vision and purpose behind your brand will shape every decision you make, from the product development process to marketing strategies. Chapter 1, *Beyond Trends - Building Timeless Value*, sets the stage by encouraging you to look beyond fleeting fashion trends and focus on creating a brand that offers lasting value. The key to success here is authenticity. By aligning your brand with values such as sustainability, inclusivity, or cultural preservation, you can build a loyal customer base that shares your vision. This authenticity allows you to create a deeper connection with your audience, making your brand resonate on a much more profound level.

In chapter 2, *From Why to Vision*, you'll learn how to define your brand's core purpose—its "why." Simon Sinek's Golden Circle framework provides a powerful tool for structuring your messaging and ensuring that your brand's vision remains clear and aligned with your values. Whether you're focusing on environmental impact or cultural storytelling, understanding and communicating the purpose behind your brand is essential for differentiating yourself in a crowded market.

Once you've identified your "why" and vision, chapter 3, *From Idea to MVP – Building the foundation*, takes you through the process of developing a Minimum Viable Product (MVP). By focusing on a simplified version of your product, you can quickly test and validate ideas without overcommitting to an unproven concept. This lean approach ensures that you are both cost-effective and market-ready, allowing you to pivot and refine your product based on real customer feedback.

The final chapter in Part 1, *Threads of Connection: Crafting a Brand Story That Resonates*, emphasizes the importance of storytelling in building an emotional connection with your audience. Your brand story should be authentic, relatable, and consistent across all touchpoints. When done right, storytelling creates a sense of community and customer loyalty, helping your brand stand out in a saturated market.

Part 2 of the book focuses on positioning, launching, and refining your product. This phase is where many brands falter, but with the right strategies, you can successfully position your product in the market, differentiate your brand from competitors, and create a meaningful connection with consumers. The chapter on *The Power of Product Positioning* shows how differentiation and value-based strategies can be powerful tools in establishing your brand's unique identity.

As the book moves into Part 3, *scaling*, you'll gain insights into how to grow your brand sustainably and efficiently. Scaling is not just about increasing production—it's about ensuring operational efficiency, market expansion, and technological integration. This section discusses using emerging technologies like AI, blockchain, and IoT to streamline processes, reduce waste, and improve inventory management. You'll also learn how to expand into new markets, diversify your product line, and build a strong community around your brand to foster long-term growth.

In addition to practical business strategies, this book emphasizes the importance of leadership, culture, and team building in scaling your brand. A strong leadership team that aligns with the brand's core values and positive work culture is essential for fostering innovation and sustaining growth.

Whether you're in the early stages of developing your brand or ready to take it to the next level, 'Build and Grow Your Fashion

Brand' offers a step-by-step guide to turning your vision into reality. Focusing on authenticity, sustainable practices, and the use of agile methodologies, this book will help you build a fashion brand that not only meets the needs of today's consumers but also thrives for years to come.

By combining actionable insights, real-world examples, and strategic frameworks, this book is the ultimate resource for fashion entrepreneurs ready to embark on a journey towards building a lasting brand. From concept to creation, launch to scale, 'Build and Grow Your Fashion Brand' will inspire you to take bold steps and build a brand that stands the test of time.

Introduction

The fashion industry isn't just about clothing, identity, expression, and innovation. Yet, launching a brand in today's fast-paced market can feel like navigating a storm. From the rise of direct-to-consumer models to the pressure for sustainability, fashion is as much about strategy as it is about style. This book is your playbook, guiding you from ideation, Minimum Viable Product, and branding to execution and scaling up. I am writing this book to provide a holistic approach for one who wants to be an entrepreneur in the fashion industry. The reason is that with nearly 3 decades of industry experience and learning each day from the industry, people, professors, and veterans, I have inspirations from many of my friends who started their entrepreneurship journey, stopped in the middle, and could not continue. So, in this book, I have ensured you get all the input and ideas required for a brand's success.

The global fashion market is projected to reach $1.7 trillion by 2026, as per Statista, with niche and sustainable brands driving this growth. When I talk about sustainability, I am sure it will become a norm in the coming years, as we are in the era of AI where information flow is swift and available to nooks and corners of the world. People are becoming aware of what they are wearing and eating. Customers no longer buy products; they invest in stories, values, and experiences. This era presents a golden opportunity for entrepreneurs to carve out their space in this competitive yet rewarding landscape.

In today's world, conventional manufacturing and linear supply chains in the fashion industry are evolving significantly.

Robots are replacing traditional labour roles, sustainability is gaining momentum in business strategy, and anyone can transform waste into raw materials and start a business. Designers are using these recycled products to create excellent apparel and accessories.

Mustafa Suleyman's excellent book, The Coming Wave, predicts "everything will change in the 21st century." Soon, we may be living with many AIs around us. They will carry out complex tasks, operate businesses, and produce unlimited digital content. The new AI wave started in the 1950s and will make the new generation the most productive in human history. This wave is improving and getting better every day. The adoption of AI will be so swift that we will all use it in one way or another in the coming years.

Fashion businesses face challenges and opportunities beyond keeping up with these advancements. They navigate complex geopolitical landscapes, responding to changing trade policies, labour laws, and higher borrowing costs amid key elections and geopolitical shifts. When I write this book, the US elections are over, and a new government has already been elected.

Technological advancements like AI, sustainability demands, and evolving consumer preferences are becoming standard business concerns as we enter new decades. The need for rapid production and transparency has intensified. According to the World Bank's 2024 projections, this period may see the worst global economic growth in three decades.

Agile and tech-savvy business responses to these changes are crucial for survival.

With all these geopolitical shifts and technological advancements and the change in the mindset of newer generations, what makes your Brand different? Pause for a moment. Jot down your answer. Is it sustainability, inclusivity, or an untapped market need? Is this the "why" of your Brand, which we'll uncover in chapter 2? As many of us know, the concept of why for businesses or entrepreneurs, which Mr. Simon Sinek popularised in his book Start with Why? The importance of understanding and communicating an organisation's or individual's "why" - their core purpose, belief, or reason for existence - as the key to inspiring and motivating others, rather than simply focusing on "what" they do or "how" they do it.

As Eric Ries says in his book the Lean Startup, "One creates a business where the customer is willing to buy. The business is not sustainable if your product does not solve a customer's problem."

As Peter Thiel says, any startup that copies another business or idea is not called a startup; it is just an improvement over an existing business. Startup founders have no guarantee of success, but they have immense confidence in their ideas and vision, and with their continuous grit and perseverance, they achieve success.

If one must be successful and happy, then I want to mention the few golden words from the book Ikigai; the author of the book says what you love (your passion), what the world needs (your mission), what you are good at (your vocation), and what you can get paid for (your profession). The author takes us on this search along with them and makes us understand how the people of Japan have been living a long and happy life. If you want to be successful in life, happy, and healthy, then you must know your Ikigai, your inner passion, which makes you work for any number of hours without feeling tired and enjoy every moment at that job. I want you to discover your passion and ask yourself why you want to create a fashion brand. If you find that your purpose in life is working in the fashion business and always want to do that work, then you can think of creating a fashion brand. Each of us must be sure of what makes us happy even after working longer hours and keep the same energy and momentum, come what may.

Michael E. Gerber says in his book The E Myth Revisited that many professionals get dissatisfied with their managers and their organisation's working culture and start thinking that they have so much experience and because of them, only their company is running. In that hallucination, they start their own business. Soon after a few months, they realise it is not their cup of coffee. Enthusiasm has dried up, and creating a business requires a different mindset than an employee, the work culture, the systems and processes, and the store's customer experiences. Business is a product. The business needs the best employees, skilled technicians, and designers. Each of these individuals may not be a successful businessperson if they think that their skills are enough to operate the business. Running a business has many aspects; one should understand those before jumping into entrepreneurship.

As the author says in the book Ikigai, know your inner passion and discover what makes you happy. Please ask yourself why you want to create a fashion brand and why me. What problem am I solving for the customer? Are there any unmet needs of the customer that I want to solve? Or am I creating a niche segment in fashion with a demand from a segment of customers? Please ask yourselves these questions before working on your idea or business.

Once you know your passion and understand why you want to create your business in fashion to pursue your idea, please ask these questions yourself:

1. Do you know your target audience's most significant pain point?
2. Can you define your Brand's mission in one sentence?
3. Are you ready to adapt and pivot quickly in response to market trends?

If you answered "no" to any of these, don't worry. This book will address the step-by-step procedures. I have responded to most of your questions about creating a fashion business. These steps can also be applied to any startup. As I have worked extensively in the Apparel Industry, I have taken many examples from this industry.

Building a fashion brand isn't just about selling clothes—it's about making an impact. As Coco Chanel said, *"Fashion is not something that exists in dresses only. Fashion is in the sky, in the street."* Let this book guide you in creating something timeless, impactful, and undeniably yours. If it helps your business or idea, then my intention of coming up with this book is accomplished.

In today's world, anything generalised or already available is given the least importance. This is like the value we provide for the most essential elements on Earth: Air, Water, and Mother Earth. We take them for granted and value them the least. As one of Kannada's oldest and most well-known poets, Gopala Krishna Adiga, says, "Life is leaving everything we have and craving what we don't have."

So, in Fashion, a purpose-driven brand isn't just reacting to what's hot right now; it's crafting an identity that resonates with consumers on a fundamental level. Take sustainability, for example; brands that prioritise eco-conscious practices are attracting a growing number of consumers who care deeply about the environment. By focusing on sustainability, these brands aren't only reducing their ecological footprint and positioning themselves as leaders who stand for a better future. This approach draws in customers who want their purchases to align with their values, fostering brand loyalty and advocacy.

Similarly, a brand that centres around cultural impact or preserves craftsmanship gives its products timeless quality. In doing so, it cultivates a story that resonates across generations. When your “why” is rooted in something as profound as cultural preservation or community empowerment, you invite customers to become part of a movement rather than just another fashion cycle.

Committing to a strong “why” can lead to a longer lifecycle for your brand. It gives customers a reason to return season after season, not for the latest trend but for the values reflected in your work. By focusing on purpose over trend, you’re building more than a fashion label—you’re building a brand with the resilience and adaptability to thrive in a constantly shifting market.

Different sets of people would start a business in the fashion industry. For young entrepreneurs who are just out of college and want to pursue their ideas, there would be some experienced professionals from the industry. Each must go through a particular set of procedures to create a brand. As Michael E. Gerber says in his book The E Myth Revisited, thinking that we have experience as a designer, business head, sourcing, or marketing professional, it would be easy to create the brand would not work. Creating a business is a product. It involves rigorous exercise. Gerber emphasises the importance of systems and processes in small businesses and distinguishing between working on the business versus in it.

We are seeing a lot of new brands emerging in the niche segments targeting the Millennials and Gen Z customers. Their focus is fast-fashion and creating differentiated products that big brands are not serving. Even brands like Zara and H&M, who are known for making fast-fashion and known for coming up with a new collection every month, especially in Zara, are not able to understand the psyche of the new generations, and that is why the new online brands like Urban Monkey, Huemn, The Souled Store, etc., are becoming successful in the online space. Slowly, they have even expanded into offline stores. In

I have provided a detailed roadmap for starting a business in the fashion world. The procedure would be the same for starting any business, like knowing the customer's pain points, asking why, and the purpose for creating a business, vision, and mission statements, product development, MVP, go-to-market strategies, etc. I have also emphasised many examples from the industry of successful people and the reasons behind their success. It will help you understand why you must create a long-lasting business and the critical non-negotiable areas you must go through before starting a brand, launching, and post-launch.

Let's get started. Your fashion legacy awaits.

known for making fast fashion and known for coming up with a new collection every month, especially in Zara, are not able to understand the psyche of the new generations, and that is why the new online brands like Urban Monkey, Huemn, The Souled Store, etc., are becoming successful in the online space. Now, they have even expanded into offline stores.

I have provided a detailed roadmap for starting a business in the fashion world. The procedure would be the same for starting any business, like knowing the customer's pain points, asking why, and the purpose for creating a business, vision, and mission statements, product development, MVP, go-to-market strategies, etc. I have also highlighted many [illegible] including [illegible]

[illegible] and the critical non-negotiable areas you must go through before starting a brand, launching, and scaling it.

Part One

NURTURING THE IDEA

Chapter 1

Beyond Trends – Building Timeless Value

"Style is very personal. It has nothing to do with fashion. Fashion is over quickly. Style is forever." – Ralph Lauren.

Fashion trends come and go, but the brands that leave a lasting impact go beyond chasing fleeting fads. They create something deeper—timeless value. Think of your Brand as a tree. Trends are like leaves that change with the seasons, but your roots—your purpose and values—must be firmly planted to withstand any storm. Fashion trends are changing more quickly than anticipated. The emergence of AI and the new generation Z (people born between 1995-2012) in their mid-20s to 30s have different aspirations than generation X and millennials. New niche brands are launched in Fashion, promoting a distinctive trend. Even the Gen Z people are accepting the new brands, which are growing rapidly. I want to compare these new Gen Z brands to technological changes in electronics and the digital space, where technology keeps changing. I can quote many examples in this space, including Motorola, Nokia, Blackberry, etc. These brands ruled the world at one point, but when technology changed swiftly, they could not upgrade and change with the technologies. New entrants who were faster and better in the new technologies and innovation took over them. I assume the same may happen to Gen Z brands entering the fashion space and sticking to fast-changing trends. If these new brands do not adapt to quick changes, they will also become obsolete. As the trend changes rapidly, adapting to newer trends is also necessary. If a company or Brand entirely depends on technology, innovation, and rapid adaptation are immaterial. As technology evolves rapidly, new entrants will capture the market if the Brands in the technology space do not keep inventing.

Microsoft was one of the biggest brands at one time. We saw how Facebook and Amazon came out on top, and then Apple commanded the number one position in the Nasdaq; now, Nvidia is leading the chart and has become the number one company in market capitalisation. Tomorrow, another new company or brand will emerge, take over Nvidia, and become number one. This phenomenon clearly shows the rapid change in technology and the quick adaptation by the industry and consumers.

Regarding the fashion world in India, legacy brands like Louis Philippe, Allen Solly, Van Heusen, Arrow, etc., have been in the industry for more than 3-4 decades and still sustain a certain percentage of market share. However, the growth in these brands has come down and become almost flat in terms of year-on-year revenues. There is competition from new international brands like Zara, H&M, Uniqlo, Massimo Dutti, Superdry, etc. Even though individual customers' affordability of branded apparel in India has increased, the growth of the Indian legacy brands has become stagnant. I consider yearly 10-15% growth stagnant or flat as inflation and GDP growth add up to 12-13%.

Some new players in the online space are Wrogn, Urban Monkey, Bewakoof, etc. These companies started purely online and created differentiated merchandise unavailable from traditional brands. Unless these new brands continuously innovate their offerings, new brands will emerge and take over the existing brands.

To begin with, if you want to start your business in fashion, you must consider the following points.

Purpose: Why does your Brand exist? When there are so many fashion brands, why would a customer want to buy your brand products? What is the unique differentiation you're bringing that is in demand? Are you solving any customer problems? Is your product designed for a particular segment of customers like Outdoor, Sports, Partywear, Ethnic, Athleisure, motorcycle, etc? Patagonia talks about finding your purpose and following it with all your heart to live a happy and satisfying life.

If I Google "purpose-driven brands" worldwide, here it comes up.

It is evident that each of these brands is different, and they have defined their purpose very clearly. They are not doing what everyone else does but sticking to their core purpose.[11]

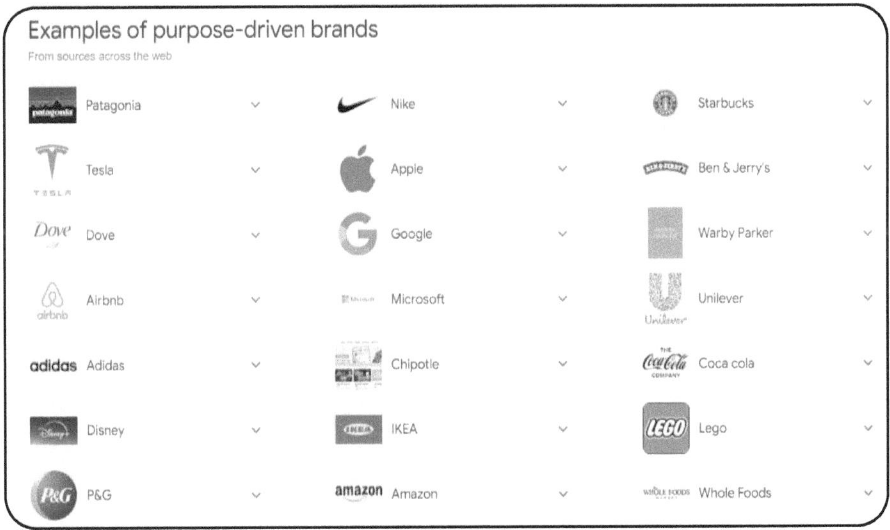

1 Image courtesy of google.com

Quality Over Quantity

> *"The bitterness of poor quality remains long after the sweetness of low price is forgotten." – Benjamin Franklin.*

All the successful brands and big organisations have always given importance and commitment to the quality of the product or service rather than quantity. I still remember that my slippers would get broken every few months when I was very young. My father decided to go for a quality product from a reputed brand, and the first name that came to his mind was Bata. The choices were also limited to Liberty or Bata. So, he gave me money to go and buy a pair of slippers of my choice. I still remember the pair of slippers I bought from Bata that lasted for over 18 months to 2 years, and that was my first and best experience of a quality product from childhood. It made a mark in my mind, and many theories started working in my mind, stating that if a brand must be successful in the long run, it is because of the consistent quality of the product.

Later, when I started working for a textile mill immediately after completing my Diploma in textile Technology before I pursued my Engineering, the export-oriented unit near Hoskote, Silktex Limited (no longer in operation), I was moulded entirely by the priority for quality in the textile industry. As the fabrics were 100% silk and ultra-premium fabrics exported to Europe and the Americas, the quality standards maintained were the highest in the industry. I worked in the weaving department and monitored the production and quality of the shift. The quality parameters, starting from the Yarn, Dyeing, and weaving, were one of the best in the industry. Later, when I moved on to another EOU unit, I could see the same standards maintained for the fabrics exported to many European countries.

Many successful brands worldwide are committed to providing quality products and services. I cannot remember any successful brand without providing quality products. Hermès creates and manufactures quality objects designed to last, be passed on from one generation to the next, and be repaired. This approach requires considering these issues at every stage, from design to sales.

Hermès prioritises using the finest materials and traditional artisan techniques to produce its leather goods, silk scarves, and other products, ensuring exceptional quality and longevity. By intentionally limiting the production of certain popular items, like the Birkin bag, Hermès creates a sense of scarcity and exclusivity, further driving demand and perceived value. Unlike many luxury brands, Hermès relies on subtle and understated marketing campaigns, focusing on the brand's inherent quality and heritage rather than celebrity endorsements.

Sustainability as a Value: The modern consumer is increasingly eco-conscious. Offering sustainable options not only aligns with customer values but also secures your relevance in the long-term. Sustainability is not just a trend in the fashion industry; it is becoming a fundamental pillar for success, particularly for new entrepreneurs.

Modern consumers, particularly Millennials and Gen Z, actively seek brands that align with their values, including sustainability, ethical practices, and environmental stewardship. Sustainable products can build trust and loyalty, ensuring repeat business and strong word-of-mouth recommendations.

Sustainability provides a Unique Selling Proposition (USP) in a crowded market where many brands offer similar products. A sustainable approach offers compelling narratives around craftsmanship, ethics, and impact, which resonate deeply with consumers. Governments and trade bodies are increasingly enforcing stricter environmental regulations. Building sustainability into your business immediately ensures compliance and avoids costly adjustments later.

As the fashion industry moves towards more eco-friendly standards, early adoption positions your brand as a leader rather than a follower. Incorporating recycling, upcycling, or take-back programmes can create additional differentiation while reducing waste. Working with sustainable textiles, such as organic cotton, recycled polyester, or bio-fabricated leather, can position your brand as forward-thinking and innovative.

While many brands in the industry talk about sustainability and launch new marketing campaigns, I have a strong feeling about their commitment to the environment. Sustainability is becoming a collection and big marketing campaign for brands rather than something done and returned to Mother Earth.

Many big brands have not implemented basic requirements like avoiding one-time plastic bags. Corn starch poly bag options are available. Still, they cost a few more to save a few cents. Brands are not adopting biodegradable corn starch poly bags that decompose into the earth within 180 days compared to the standard poly bags, which take around 1000 years!

The same goes for the use of FSC packaging,

The brands are not adopting FSC packaging as it costs a few cents more. My question to Popular Brands is, what is the commitment to generating carbon footprints? Are they committed to giving back to the environment?

Therefore, your sustainable offerings and commitment to giving back to Mother Earth will become increasingly critical. If, as a founder, you are committed to designing your products and packaging sustainably, then the legacy will continue in the coming years. I urge all existing and new brands to thoroughly inculcate sustainable processes in their mission and vision statements.

Cultural Relevance: Brands like Levi's have adapted over centuries without losing their core identity, proving you can evolve while staying authentic. Leveraging cultural themes allows you to differentiate your brand in a competitive market. Highlighting multicultural influences showcases inclusivity and appeals to global or diverse audiences. Drawing inspiration from cultural heritage, art, and history can create distinctive designs and products.

Some diverse cultures and traditions have been practiced in India for thousands of years. In each region in India, there has been a change in the language, culture, and ethnicity. The food you will get from North India differs entirely from Southern India, and the same holds true for East and West. Various traditional textile product preparation methods are carried out in these regions. I have personally seen how Southern India is famous for silk Sarees, where you will find different varieties of silk sarees in Kanchi, Dharmavaram, Molaklmuru, etc. Similarly, if you visit Rajasthan, the kind of textile apparel is wholly based on other types of prints applied to cotton fabrics. Indigo prints are widely used in the Rajasthan region.

In India, FabIndia is one of the brands that ingrained cultural diversity and projected artisans' cultural values and empowerment. I have done a lot of shopping at FabIndia, and the authentic fabric and prints make it different and distinctive from other brands. As the brand constantly markets its commitment and resonates stories on a deeper level of human expression, one would want to stay connected and loyal. Fab India never changes the fabrics and prints in its offerings; unlike any known brand products, the merchandise of FabIndia would not shrink or fade after the first wash, but customers know that the authentic products behave similarly, so when the brand constantly serves the products and communicates authenticity, naturally customers would get associated with the brand.

To incorporate cultural relevance in your brand:

1. Study the history, traditions, and values of the cultures you wish to include.
2. Analyse the preferences and behaviours of your target audience through surveys, focus groups, or trend analysis.
3. Collaborate with local artisans, designers, or cultural experts to ensure authenticity.

4. Involve community members to co-create designs and narratives.
5. Use traditional techniques, materials, or motifs in a modern context.
6. Ensure that your designs and messaging honour, rather than exploit, cultural significance.
7. Engage in conversations around cultural identity, representation, and empowerment.

Take a moment to reflect: What is your brand's "why"? Could you write it down in one sentence? If it feels tied to a current trend, dig deeper. How can it resonate beyond today?

- The average lifespan of a fashion trend is just 3-5 years.
- According to a recent Deloitte study, brands with a clear purpose grow 2.5 times faster than others.

Imagine a customer holding your product years from now and still finding it meaningful. You're not just creating a brand—you're making memories, heirlooms, and a legacy.

Rihanna's Fenty Brand disrupted the beauty and fashion industries by prioritising inclusivity. Fenty Beauty launched with 40 foundation shades, redefining what timeless value means in diversity. Similarly, Fenty's lingerie focuses on body positivity, proving that inclusivity creates lasting customer loyalty.

Stella McCartney, a pioneer of sustainable fashion, has built a brand rooted in eco-friendly practices. She uses materials like organic cotton and recycled polyester. Her commitment to ethical luxury has set her apart as a timeless brand leader.

Pharrell's collaboration with Adidas focuses on individuality and self-expression. Timeless value emerges from creating designs that celebrate personal identity over passing trends. Primarily focused on their "Originals" line, where he designs sneakers and apparel with a strong emphasis on bright colours, bold patterns, and inclusive messaging, often featuring his "Human race" branding; notable releases include the "Supercolor" Stan Smith pack with 50 different colourways, the "Human Race" NMD with printed "Human Race" text, and more recent "Samba" sneakers in vibrant monochrome palettes. This partnership is recognised for its significant impact on the sneaker market due to the high demand for limited-edition releases and their resale value.

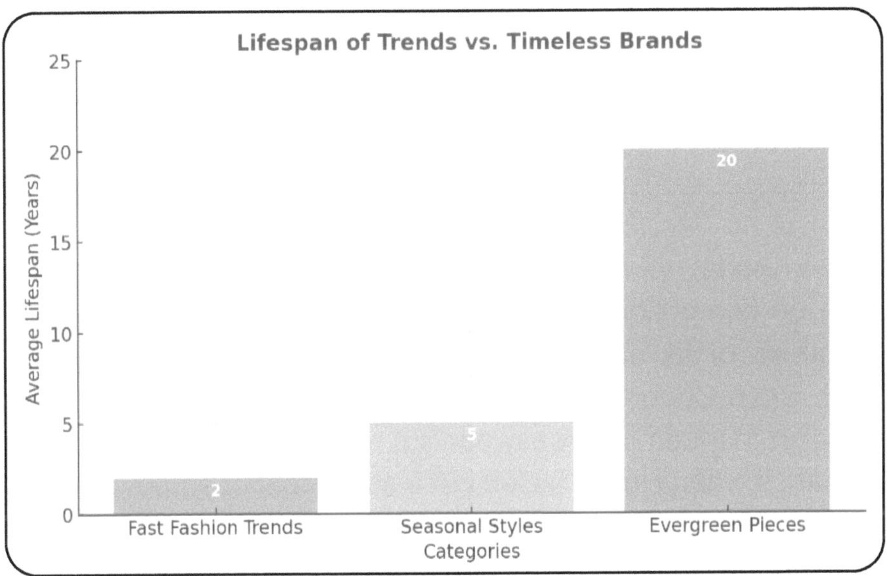

Fast-Fashion Trends: 1–3 years (average ~2 years)

Seasonal Styles: 3–7 years (average ~5 years)

Evergreen Pieces: 10–30+ years (average ~20 years)

An evolution in speed and innovation underpins three generations of fast-fashion companies.[2]

2 Image courtesy of The State of Fashion 2024/2025 from Mackisay & Company

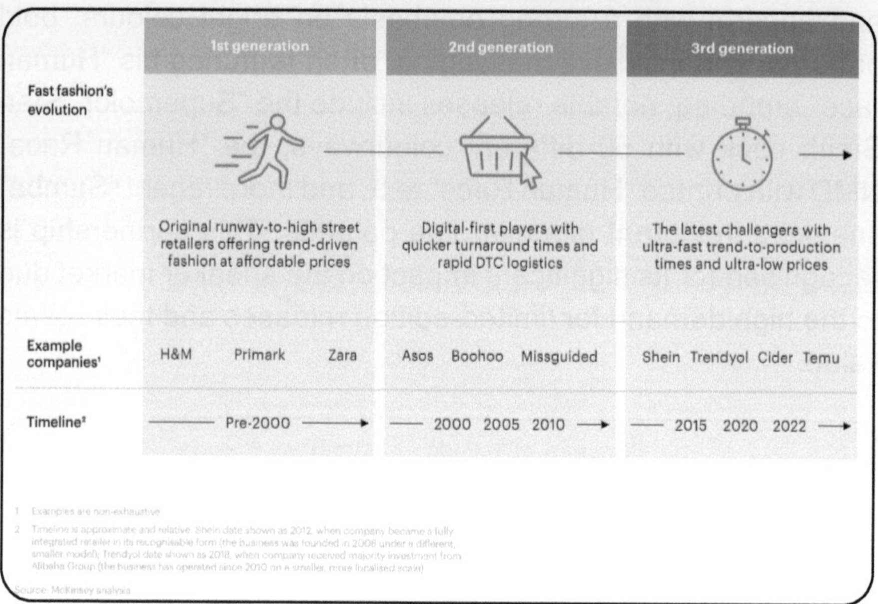

Online model to offline or omnichannel retail — what has been its competitive edge could face some dilution, and the stickiness of its core customer base may be challenged. In 1954, Coco Chanel introduced the iconic Chanel tweed jacket, a design inspired by menswear but reimagined for the modern woman. It wasn't just a jacket but a statement of empowerment, functionality, and elegance. Decades later, this piece remains a symbol of timelessness, worn by icons like Princess Diana and reimagined by contemporary celebrities such as Margot Robbie. What made it timeless? It wasn't just the design but the story of innovation, individuality, and enduring relevance.

Timeless brands don't chase the spotlight – they create their own. By prioritising authenticity, quality, and purpose, you can build a legacy that endures long after trends fade. One of the best examples I can give here is Hush Puppies. As Malcolm Gladwell said in the book Tipping Point, the brand was not doing well for many years; many new brands in the industry were gaining good growth and had become the talk of the town. But Hush Puppies never budged from their core identities and standards. One fine day, the new traditional look and styling trend started gaining momentum, and Hush Puppies came into the limelight. From there, Hush Puppies has never looked back and gained the name for the most comfortable shoes available worldwide. Despite the competition and changes in the trends, Hush Puppies stayed true to their core style and looks.

One of the most critical points in creating a brand is to ask,

“What problems are you solving for the customer?”

How are you going to improve the customer’s life?”

To build a brand that stands the test of time, think beyond what’s trending and consider what will matter tomorrow. The roots of your brand’s legacy start here. When I joined the Motorcycle Apparel Brand after working for nearly 2 decades in contemporary legacy brands, the first instruction from our Business Head and the Management was to.[3]

---

3 Image courtesy McKinsey & Company from the article “The State of Fashion 2024/2025”

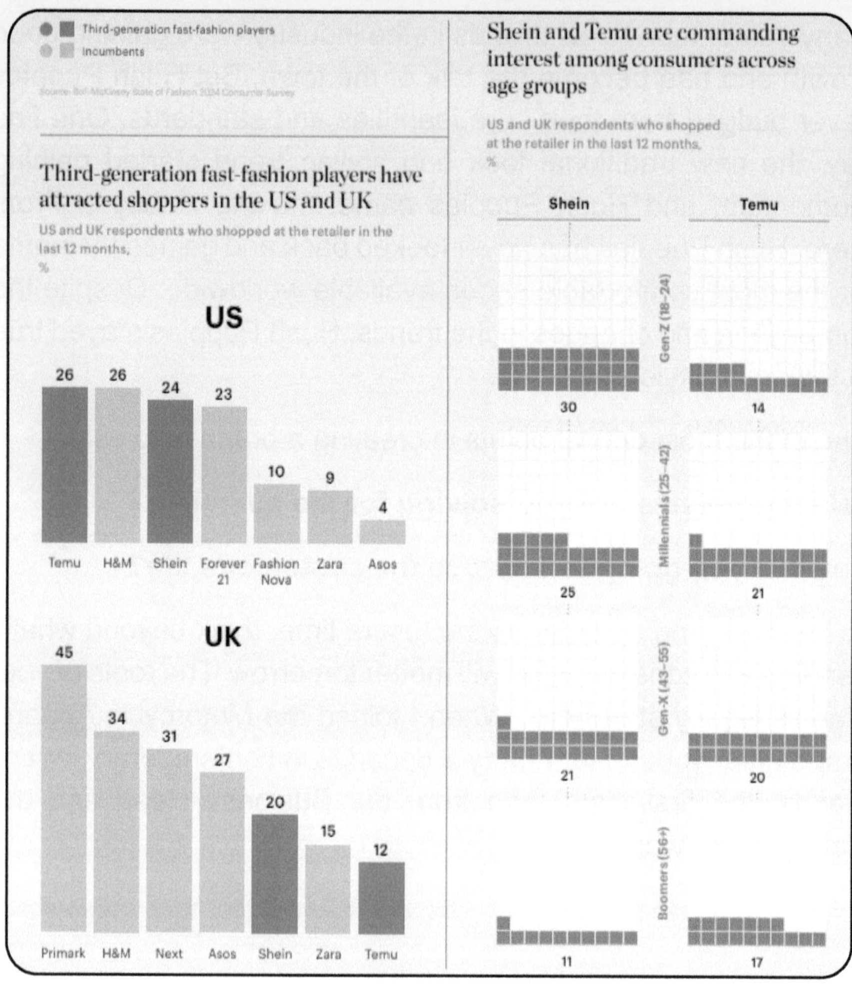

Keep the products distinctive and do not follow the trend. Trends change every season; if we follow trends, we must keep reinventing new fits, fabrics, and styles every season. We must also keep evolving with the changes in the industry dynamics. However, there is a difference between growing with the industry dynamics and adapting to the fashion trends. Trends change rapidly. Yesterday, it was all Skinny-fit denim; today, you have the trend of torn jeans, and tomorrow, you may come up with baggy or completely loose denim like the loose-fit T-shirts and sweatshirts that are in trend now. First, we must create an identity for the brand. If one keeps adapting to the changing fashion trends, the core brand identity gets compromised. You may take a few details from the new fashion trends, but the brand's core identity should remain the same.

A few recent examples of brands that stuck to their brand identities and created their niche are Rare Rabbit, Chumbak, FabIndia, Manyavar, W, Aurelia, and many more in the ethnic wear segment. The above brands identified their niche and introduced products only to that segment. They have not tried to do everything that every other brand is doing; they stuck to their core identity and look for the brand.

The typical fashion brands in India and internationally work on the Spring, Summer, Autumn, and Winter seasons. Some brands follow 4 seasons, dividing the seasons every 3 months, and some follow 3 seasons by keeping festive as a separate season. In India, October and November are the festive seasons, and Dasara/Durga Puja and Deepavali festivals are celebrated all over India in a big way. So, most legacy brands want to encash this festive season when most buying will happen throughout the country. Brands create vibrant, colourful merchandise suitable for these festivals. A typical brand in India works similarly.

However, as the author, Mr. Anindya Ray, a fashion industry veteran with experience working for most of the luxury brands in India, says in his book Fashion Fables, "Is the season still relevant today?" Fashion designers and WGSN release the colours for every season. Is it still relevant? With the emergence of new online fast-fashion brands, we are seeing the new generations accept niche and differentiated fashion.

So, with all the uncertainties and changing geopolitical scenarios, the world is cautious about developing any new product from third-world countries. Prominence is given to the products produced in their own countries; even if the product is expensive, the people want to promote the products made in their own country. After COVID-19, the world has learned how dependent each country is on another. When China was in lockdown for more than a year, the whole world suffered due to the necessity of products. Vessels got jam-packed at Shanghai ports, and the shortage of containers skyrocketed the freight costs. China taught the world that they are the factory for the world. Now, countries are looking at the China +1 option for their products. Many orders may have moved from China to countries like Vietnam, Indonesia, Bangladesh, India, and some other beneficiaries.[4]

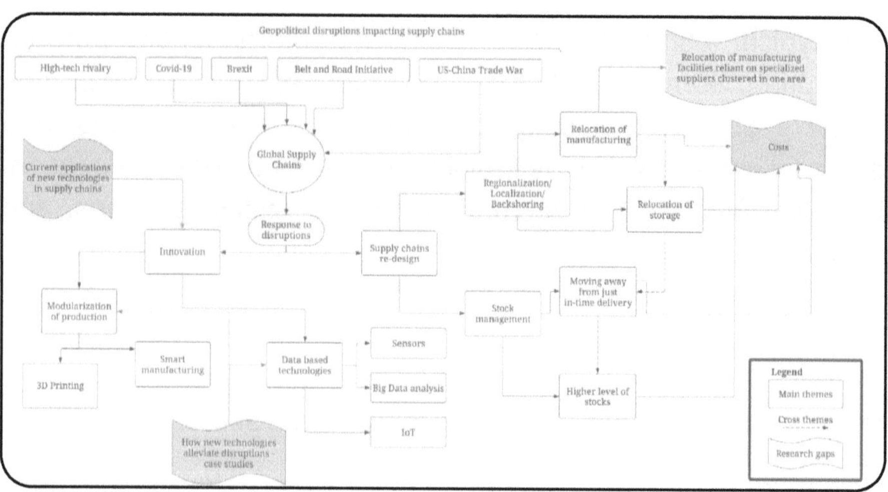

The figure shows the result of mapping geopolitical impacts on supply chains. Geopolitical events affect supply chains. On the one hand, this impact leads to technological innovation through disruption, and on the other hand, it leads to efforts to redesign the existing supply chains.

---

4 **Geopolitical disruptions in global supply chains: a state-of-the-art literature review**
Lukasz Bednarski, Roscoe, Constantin & Martin C. Schleper Received 24 Aug 2022, Accepted 13 Nov 2023, Published online: 01 Dec 2023

This insight strongly signals that many Asian countries will shift production from China. As the textile ecosystem develops in these countries, it will help with new product development and innovation.

One of the critical aspects before starting any business is to understand the pain points of the customer.

To know the problem statement of the customer, Sara Beckman, a faculty member at UC Berkeley's Haas School of Business, talks about ethnographic interviews. Ethnographic interviews are a powerful tool for researchers seeking to uncover deep insights into human behaviour and cultural patterns. By asking the right questions, researchers can delve into the lived experiences, beliefs, and values that shape individuals and communities.

Suppose you have an idea or experience in fashion design and want to start your fashion brand. In that case, first, you must consider how your product would differ from the products already available in the market. What problem are you going to solve for the customer? Is there a similar product already available in the market? Please conduct ethnographic interviews to understand the customers' pain points. Ethnographic interviews are invaluable for researchers aiming to uncover profound insights into human behaviour and cultural dynamics. This approach allows interviewees to express themselves freely, revealing nuanced perspectives that might remain hidden.

The art of conducting compelling ethnographic interviews is creating a comfortable atmosphere and asking open-ended questions that encourage detailed narratives.

If you want to find out the real problems in the world, you can conduct ethnographic interviews.

A guide for 15 thoughtful questions to evoke rich, meaningful participant responses is provided. Utilising the questions enables researchers to explore the lived experiences, beliefs, and values that influence individuals and communities.

The key to conducting successful ethnographic interviews is fostering a comfortable environment and posing open-ended questions that invite detailed narratives. This approach empowers interviewees to freely share their perspectives, revealing subtle nuances that might remain concealed. Consider how the questions can be tailored to fit various research contexts and cultural settings, resulting in more comprehensive and genuine ethnographic data.

Ethnographic interviews are a robust qualitative research method to gain deep insights into people's lives, cultures, and experiences. Unlike traditional interviews, these in-depth conversations allow researchers to immerse themselves in the participant's world, uncovering rich, contextual information that might remain hidden. By combining observation with open-ended questioning, ethnographic interviews provide a holistic understanding of individuals and communities.

The key to successful ethnographic interviews is creating a relaxed, conversational atmosphere where participants feel comfortable sharing their stories and perspectives. Researchers often conduct these interviews in the participant's natural environment, such as the home or workplace, to capture authentic behaviours and interactions. This approach enables the interviewer to gather verbal responses, cues, and environmental factors, contributing to a more comprehensive understanding of the subject matter.

A practical ethnographic interview guide[5] is crucial for conducting insightful research. To create a comprehensive guide, consider the following key elements:

5 From the article 15 ethnographic interviews with examples from insight7.io

Your ethnographic interview will help you gather rich, meaningful data while maintaining respect for your participants' cultural contexts.

You can prepare practical questions

It is crucial to ask the right questions for the success of the ethnographic interview. There should be a balance between open-ended exploration and focused probing. Cultural context and research objectives become essential in the interview. You can start with broad, descriptive questions encouraging participants to share their opinions freely. As the interview progresses, you can dig deeper with more specific questions that address the research goals. You should pay attention to the non-verbal cues and adapt questions based on the responses.

As an entrepreneur aiming to establish a fashion brand, conducting thorough ethnographic interviews can provide invaluable insights into your target market. This process will help you understand consumer behaviour, preferences, and pain points, essential for creating a brand that resonates with your audience.

Understanding Your Market

Start by utilising open-ended questions to gather detailed information about your potential customers. Instead of asking, "Do you like fashion?" consider asking, "Can you describe a typical shopping experience?"

Another critical strategy is active listening. Pay close attention to the responses and use follow-up questions to delve deeper. Phrases like "That's fascinating, could you tell me more about that?" or "What led you to feel that way?" encourage participants to provide richer insights. The most valuable information often comes when interviewees freely reflect and share their thoughts.

Developing a Comprehensive Interview Guide

Here are some example questions to guide your ethnographic interviews for your fashion brand:

- 'Can you describe a typical day in your life?'
- 'What are some of your favourite fashion brands and why?'
- 'How do you typically shop for clothing and accessories?'
- 'What challenges do you face when shopping for fashion items?'
- 'Can you recount a recent purchase experience that was particularly satisfying or frustrating?'
- 'What influences your fashion choices?'
- 'How do trends and seasons affect your shopping habits?'
- 'What do you value most in a fashion brand?'

These questions will help you understand consumer behaviour, preferences, and the factors influencing their shopping decisions.

Uncovering Consumer Insights

Craft questions that explore daily routines, cultural influences, and personal preferences to gain deeper insights into consumer behaviour. For example, you might ask, "How do your daily activities influence your fashion choices?" or "What cultural or social factors impact your style?"

Observe non-verbal cues and body language during these discussions to gain further context. By combining thoughtful questioning techniques with keen observation, you can uncover hidden insights that shape consumer behaviour.

Analysing the Data

After conducting the interviews:

1. Transcribe the audio or video recordings to create written records.

2. Organise the transcribed data systematically, categorising responses based on themes or questions.
3. Utilise data management software to assist in organising and coding the data.

Identify patterns, themes and key insights. These will help you understand the data's underlying meanings and connections.

Conduct a thematic analysis to identify recurring themes and patterns in the data. Combine data from multiple sources to validate your findings and enhance the credibility of your research.

Prepare a detailed report summarising the insights gained from the interviews. Use this information to develop a brand strategy that aligns with consumer needs and preferences.

Implementing Your Findings

Translate the insights into actionable strategies for your fashion brand. Focus on creating a unique value proposition, developing marketing campaigns, and designing products that resonate with your target audience.

Present your findings to stakeholders and collaborators, using visual aids to illustrate key insights. Gather feedback and reflect on the research process to continuously improve your brand strategy.

From the founder of Gen AI digital disruptor accelerator startup Tiny Magiq, we gain invaluable insights on nurturing an idea and the inception of startups. What drives the psyche of these founders? Do successful founders possess unique traits or a different way of thinking? Dr. Sukumar affirms that they do. He describes this unique attribute as a problem-solving mindset. Unlike ordinary individuals, these founders confront crises or problems by actively seeking solutions and taking decisive actions.

Consider Travis Kalanick, who, stranded on a snowy evening in Paris, unable to find a taxi, recognised the daily struggle faced by many in securing a cab. This realisation spurred him into action, leading to the creation of Uber in 2009.

While many are familiar with the bird's-eye view, startups must adopt a worm's-eye view. One must delve deeper into one's actions to understand the customer and their behaviour. For instance, if you plan to open a Korean cuisine restaurant in a city with a unique offering, you must study similar restaurants. Observe the customer's journey and identify pain points encountered during their visits. How can the customer experience be streamlined and enhanced?

Start with the parking area: Is there enough space? How does the customer enter the restaurant? Is there a pre-booking system, or do they wait for a table? What is the ambiance like? Every minor detail must be scrutinised, from the aroma and seating to how waitstaff greet the customers. Identifying and addressing these pain points is crucial for the success of startups. Dr Sukumar aptly calls this the Worm's Eye View, focusing on the minutiae that make a significant impact.

According to an article titled "This is the Key to Breakthrough Innovation," 3M scientists emphasise that innovation is often misinterpreted as solitary scientists in a lab achieving a breakthrough moment. Successful innovation arises from collaboration, curiosity, and linking seemingly unrelated concepts. Scientist Audrey Sharman, who holds the most patents of any woman at 3M, acknowledges that she did not achieve her successes alone. At 3M, innovation is a team effort. The company frequently organises tech forums across various divisions, allowing scientists to exchange ideas about challenges and setbacks. While having ideas is essential, translating those ideas into innovative products that benefit people, or the company, is crucial for progress.

Timeless brands are like lighthouses – they don't move with the tides but stand firm, guiding others through the waves.

As Ralph Lauren once said: *"I don't design clothes. I design dreams."*

You're not just creating a fashion brand but building a legacy. Make it timeless.

Action Items for Building a Timeless Fashion Brand

Define Your Brand's Purpose

- Clearly articulate why your Brand exists beyond making profits. Align with sustainability, inclusivity, or cultural preservation.

Focus on Quality Over Quantity

- Establish quality benchmarks for materials and craftsmanship. Use artisan techniques and premium materials like Hermès.

Integrate Sustainability

- Assess Materials: Explore sustainable options such as organic cotton or recycled fabrics.
- Plan Initiatives: Incorporate recycling, upcycling, or take-back programmes.

Stay Culturally Relevant

- Leverage Cultural Themes: Use authentic art, history, or traditional inspirations.

Develop a Brand Identity

- Establish Core Values: Define what sets your brand apart from trends.
- Ensure Consistency: Keep designs aligned with your core identity.

Understand Market Needs

- Conduct Ethnographic Research: Interview potential customers to uncover their pain points.

- Analyse Findings: Identify patterns and themes from interview data.

Create a Unique Value Proposition

- Address Customer Pain Points: Solve specific problems identified through research.
- Evaluate Competitors: Analyse gaps in the market.

Innovate for Longevity

- Adopt New Technologies: Stay ahead with AI-driven personalisation or sustainable production methods.
- Adapt Without Compromising Identity: Incorporate trends selectively while retaining brand ethos.

Monitor Industry Dynamics

- Evaluate Seasonal Trends: Determine the relevance of Spring/Summer or Autumn/Winter lines.
- Stay Agile: Regularly assess and respond to geopolitical or market shifts (e.g., the China +1 strategy).

Tell a Compelling Brand Story

- Highlight Legacy Potential: Imagine a future where your product becomes an heirloom.
- Connect Emotionally: Share the journey behind your product.

Validate Through Continuous Feedback

- Engage Stakeholders: Present findings from interviews and market research.

Iterate Based on Feedback: Adapt products and messaging according to customer responses.

Chapter 2

Define Your Why

"People don't buy what you do; they buy why you do it. And what you do simply proves what you believe." – Simon Sinek.

Understanding the Power of "Why": Why It Matters in Fashion

Every iconic fashion brand begins with a spark—a vision. It's that moment of inspiration, a dream that feels too big to ignore. But vision alone isn't enough. To make it a reality, you must shape it into a concrete concept, like a sculptor chiselling a masterpiece from a raw stone. The story of Michelangelo in 10x Is Easier Than 2x by Dan Sullivan and Dr. Benjamin Hardy is a powerful metaphor for achieving extraordinary outcomes by focusing on what truly matters and letting go of unnecessary distractions.

1. **Focus on What's Essential**
   - Michelangelo famously described sculpting as removing everything that wasn't part of the figure within the block of marble. Similarly, achieving great results requires identifying and concentrating on the most essential elements of your goals, eliminating everything non-essential.
2. **Simplicity is Key to Greatness**
   - Creating something extraordinary, like Michelangelo's *David*, is not about adding more complexity but about simplifying. Prioritise clarity and simplicity over the incremental approach.

3. **Vision Guides Execution**
   - Michelangelo didn't see a block of marble; he saw *David* within it. A compelling vision that defines and drives the process. This vision provides a sense of purpose and focus.
4. **Elimination of Mediocrity**
   - You must reject good opportunities and focus only on the best ones. Michelangelo's approach demonstrates the value of removing what doesn't align with the vision.
5. **Inspiration Over Hard Work**
   - While sculpting took effort, Michelangelo's inspiration and clarity of purpose made his work extraordinary.

Similarly, we must have a vision and know why we must create a Fashion Brand. Where should I focus? What is essential? How can we maintain simplicity while working on the big vision by eliminating mediocrity?

Define Your "Why"

Your vision must have a purpose. Nike's "Just Do It" wasn't just a tagline but a philosophy that inspired generations. What will your brand stand for?

Simon Sinek, the author of *Start with Why*, emphasises that great leaders and brands inspire action by clearly articulating their reasons for doing what they do. According to Sinek, the "why" is your purpose, cause, or belief—the reason your brand exists beyond making money.

Sinek's Golden Circle framework is a simple yet powerful model: It focuses on three concentric circles, starting from the inside: **Why**, **How**, and **What**. The framework emphasises that successful brands communicate from the inside-out, beginning with their "why."

Sinek explains that Apple's success isn't primarily due to the quality of its products (although they are excellent), but because of its clear and compelling **reason**. Apple exists to **challenge the status quo** and **think differently**. This purpose drives everything they do.

A typical marketing message for most companies starts with the product (What) and moves outward:

- **What:** "We make great computers."
- **How:** "They're beautifully designed and user-friendly."
- **Why:** [Implied, if addressed at all.]

In contrast, Apple communicates starting with **Why**:

1. **Why:** "Everything we do, we believe in challenging the status quo. We believe in thinking differently."
2. **How:** "We challenge the status quo by making our products beautifully designed, simple to use, and user-friendly."
3. **What:** "We just happen to make great computers. Want to buy one?"

The above message resonates deeply with consumers because it appeals to their emotions and beliefs, inspiring trust and loyalty beyond the product.

WHY (The Core)

- The purpose, cause, or belief that drives your brand. It's the reason your organisation exists beyond financial gain.
- Starting with "why" connects emotionally with your audience, builds trust, and inspires people to believe in your work.

HOW (The Process)

- The values, principles, or methods that differentiate your brand. It's how you bring your "why" to life.
- The "how" is your brand's Unique Selling Proposition (USP) or the innovative practices that set you apart.

WHAT (The Outcome)

- The tangible products or services your brand offers.
- Most organisations start with the "what," but focusing on the "why" gives your products deeper meaning.

Many companies have succeeded by clearly defining and communicating their **Why**, like Apple. Here are some other examples:

Tesla

- **Why:** To accelerate the world's transition to sustainable energy.
- **How:** By designing cutting-edge, environmentally friendly technology and making it desirable and accessible.
- **What:** Electric vehicles, solar products, and energy solutions.

Tesla doesn't just sell cars; it sells a vision of a cleaner, sustainable future. This strong sense of purpose inspires a loyal following and positions Tesla as more than just an automotive company—it's a movement towards change.

Nike

- **Why:** To bring inspiration and innovation to every athlete globally (*and as co-founder Bill Bowerman famously added, "If you have a body, you are an athlete"*).
- **How:** By creating innovative sports gear and championing stories of perseverance and triumph.
- **What:** Shoes, apparel, and sports equipment.

Nike inspires emotional connections through its storytelling, like the "Just Do It" campaign, which encourages people to overcome challenges and believe in their potential.

Patagonia

- **Why:** To save our home planet and promote environmental stewardship.
- **How:** By making sustainable, high-quality products and advocating for environmental causes.
- **What:** Outdoor clothing and accessories gear

Patagonia's dedication to sustainability, such as donating a portion of profits to environmental initiatives and encouraging customers to repair rather than replace their products, has cultivated a fiercely loyal customer base that aligns with its mission values.

IKEA

- **Why:** To create a better everyday life for the many people.
- **How:** By offering affordable, well-designed, and functional home furnishings.
- **What:** Flat-pack furniture and home accessories.

IKEA's focus on affordability and accessibility reflects its belief in democratising design, making beautiful and practical living spaces available to people of all income levels.

Starbucks

- **Why:** To inspire and nurture the human spirit—one person, one cup, and one neighbourhood at a time.
- **How:** Creating a welcoming, inclusive atmosphere and delivering exceptional coffee experiences.
- **What:** Coffee, tea, and café experiences.

Starbucks goes beyond selling coffee. Its "third place" concept fosters community and belonging by providing a space between home and work where people can relax and connect.

Airbnb

- **Why:** To create a world where anyone can belong anywhere.
- **How:** By offering unique, affordable accommodations and enabling hosts to share their homes and cultures.
- **What:** An online platform for lodging and experiences.

Airbnb focuses on belonging and experiences rather than just accommodations, positioning itself as a brand that connects people across cultures.

Why People Buy: Customers don't buy *what* you do; they buy *why* you do it.

Inside-Out Communication: Starting with your "why" creates a sense of purpose and inspires loyalty.

A recent example from the Indian rental car industry is Blue Smart Cabs, which operates only electric cars. The app they have developed depicts the amount of carbon emissions a customer has saved after taking a ride in them. This gives the customer a sense of satisfaction, and they feel happy for contributing to the environment to some extent. This is a perfect example of the vision behind why they are doing the business, how they want to contribute to the environment, and what their business is.

Market disruption may gather pace, with third generation fast-fashion companies doubling down on marketplaces to expand across categories, price points, and consumer segments. Customer engagement will likely remain a key differentiator as these players use their strong communities and gamification tactics to increase the average basket size, seeking to grow profits and safeguard a viable business model for the future. The industry could feel the effects of these third-generation players, and companies might want to note their most successful strategies to capture the modern consumer's attention.

1. Define your Brand's purpose: Why does your Brand exist?
2. Build your strategy around it: How do you design, produce, and market in alignment with your "why"?

3. Align your products with your core message: What does your product stand for in the eyes of your customers?

Understand Your Market

Your concept must address a genuine need. When Spanx launched, it wasn't just shapewear but a solution to millions of women's problems.

Understanding your market is the cornerstone of building a successful fashion brand. In today's competitive landscape, knowing your customers, competitors, and industry trends is essential for making informed decisions and creating a brand that resonates.

Research Your Audience

Your market begins with your audience. Demographic research identifies the customer's age, gender, income, and lifestyle. Similarly, Psychographic research delves deeper into customers' values, interests, and shopping behaviours. Brands like H&M conduct extensive surveys to understand shifting demands, such as changes in the shopping preferences of upcoming generations.

You can also conduct an Ideal Customer Profile (ICP) to learn what the ideal customer does on weekends and what frustrates them most about current fashion options.

Analyse Competitors

Conduct a **competitive analysis** to identify your brand's unique positioning.

- **Direct Competitors:** Brands offering similar products at similar price points.
- **Indirect Competitors:** Substitute products or services.

- **Example:** Nykaa Fashion competes with Myntra in India but differentiates by focusing on curated premium collections.
    - A McKinsey report reveals that **63% of consumers prioritise sustainability**[6] when choosing brands.
    - **88% of Indian millennials** prefer personalised shopping experiences (BCG).[7]
- Analytics tools like Google Trends or Shopify reports can be used to track purchasing behaviours.
- **Surveys:** Conduct online polls to identify customer pain points.
- **Community Engagement:** Use focus groups or online forums to build rapport with potential buyers.

Conclusion

Understanding your market is not a one-time activity but a continuous process. Brands that listen closely to their audience and adapt accordingly stand out in the competitive fashion world. As an entrepreneur, you should continuously listen to customers and watch their changing behaviours. One of the successes of implementing customer needs and priorities well is OnePlus Mobile. They engaged early adopters and tech enthusiasts in forums like XDA Developers and Reddit, gathering feedback and creating a sense of ownership and community among potential customers.

OnePlus positioned its phones as “flagship killers,” offering premium specifications (high-end processors, top-notch displays, and quality build) at nearly half the price of established flagship phones.

---

6 McKinsey report titled **“Navigating Challenging Stakeholder Expectations of Brands”** discusses consumer expectations and brand alignment

7 BCG report titled **“The $2 Trillion Opportunity: How Gen Z is Shaping the New India.”**

This disrupted the market by providing exceptional value, appealing to tech-savvy customers who wanted high performance without paying a premium. Instead of competing directly with giants like Apple or Samsung in the broader market, OnePlus targeted tech enthusiasts who valued specs, performance, and value over brand prestige.

Their early campaigns highlighted competitors' pain points (e.g. overpriced devices and lack of customisation) and offered OnePlus as the solution.

Create a Unique Identity

A strong concept resonates through its uniqueness. A brand's unique identity is its DNA—the essence that sets it apart in the crowded fashion marketplace. It's more than a logo or a tagline; it's the emotional connection customers feel with your brand. Building this identity requires deeply understanding your brand's purpose, values, and target audience.

Telfar, the New York-based fashion brand founded by Telfar Clemens in 2005, has carved out a distinctive niche in the fashion world with its radical approach to accessibility, inclusivity, and cultural resonance.

"Not for You, For Everyone": Telfar's motto encapsulates its mission to make luxury fashion inclusive rather than exclusive. Unlike traditional luxury brands that rely on scarcity and high price points, Telfar offers high-quality designs at accessible prices.

Define Your Brand Values

Your brand identity should reflect what your brand stands for—your **core values**.

- The Indian Brand **FabIndia** bases its identity on sustainability and the promotion of local craftsmanship. Every product reflects its ethos of "celebrating India's heritage."

  If my brand were a person, what values would define it?

Craft a Distinct Visual Language

Your Brand's visuals—logo, colour palette, fonts, and packaging—must evoke the right emotions.

- **Statistics:** Studies show that **80% of consumers recognise a brand by its colours** (Source: University of Loyola).
- **Example: Manish Malhotra's** brand is synonymous with opulence, reflected in his bold colour choices and intricate designs.

Storytelling: The Heart of Identity

Customers remember stories, not features.

- Share your journey: Why did you start the brand? What challenges did you overcome?

- **Example: Tata CLiQ Luxury** narrates its story as a platform that bridges global luxury brands with Indian sensibilities, emphasising exclusivity and trust.

Build Emotional Connections

Emotionally connected customers have a **306% higher lifetime value** (Motista).

- Conduct a survey: *What do customers feel when interacting with your brand?*
- Create experiences that make customers feel special, like personalised recommendations or packaging.

Stay Consistent Across Channels

Your brand should speak the same language across its website, social media, and offline stores.

- **Nykaa** consistently blends pink hues and minimalist aesthetics across all touchpoints, reinforcing its identity.

Real Life Insights

- A survey by McKinsey found that **60% of consumers choose brands that align with their values.**[8]
- **Raw Mango** incorporates handloom textiles to connect with India's cultural heritage, carving a unique niche.

Your brand's identity is its signature in the market. As Simon Sinek says, *"People don't buy what you do; they buy why you do it."* Stay authentic and let your identity resonate with your audience's values and aspirations.

---

8 McKinsey report titled **"Navigating Challenging Stakeholder Expectations of Brands"** discusses consumer expectations and brand alignment

Reflect on these questions:

- Why does my vision excite me?
- What problem does my brand solve?
- How is my concept different from competitors?

Write down your answers to start shaping your idea.

A clear vision guides decisions, attracts loyal customers, and builds resilience—a strong "why" that differentiates the brand from a crowded market.

Patagonia is deeply rooted in environmental conservation, setting it apart as one of the most mission-driven brands in the apparel industry. Founded by Yvon Chouinard, a passionate climber and environmentalist, Patagonia aims to address environmental degradation, advocating for sustainability and social responsibility within its operations and beyond. Here's how this commitment manifests and resonates with eco-conscious consumers:

A strong "why" is the foundation of every successful fashion brand. It defines the purpose beyond profit, inspires action, and builds emotional connections with the audience. Drawing from Simon Sinek's *Golden Circle framework*, the chapter emphasises starting from the core (why) and working outward (how and what) to create meaningful brand narratives.

Key Takeaways from the Chapter:

The Golden Circle Framework

- Why: The belief or purpose driving your brand.
- How: The unique methods or principles defining your process.
- What: The tangible products/services offered.

Successful brands like Apple, Tesla, and Patagonia thrive by clearly communicating their "why."

Why It Matters in Fashion

A strong "why" guides brand decisions, fosters resilience, and helps differentiate in a crowded market. It also resonates with values-driven consumers, mainly Gen Z and Millennials, who prefer authentic stories and purpose-driven brands.

Action Points for Building Your "Why"

Reflect on Your Vision

- What excites you about your brand's purpose?
- What problem are you solving for your audience?
- How does your vision stand out from competitors?

Define Your Brand's Purpose

- Align it with values that matter to you and your target audience (e.g. sustainability, inclusivity, innovation).

Communicate Your Why Clearly

- Develop messaging that starts with your "why" and flows into "how" and "what."
- Use storytelling to engage customers emotionally.

Understand Your Market

- Research audience needs and behaviours.
- Identify market gaps through competitive analysis.

Build Emotional Connections

- Ensure consistency across branding, products, and communication channels.

- Engage customers through authentic narratives and interactive platforms.

Stay Purpose-Driven

- Regularly revisit your brand's purpose to adapt while staying true to core values.

Chapter 3

From Idea to MVP – Building the Foundation

"Think Like a Tech Startup"

> *"Don't find customers for your products; find products for your customers." – Seth Godin.*

> *"The MVP is not necessarily the smallest product imaginable, but the fastest way to get through the Build-Measure-Learn feedback loop with the minimum amount of effort." – Eric Ries.*

Every great brand starts with a single spark—a bold idea. But turning that spark into a roaring fire requires strategy, focus, and action. This chapter will explore how adopting a tech startup mindset can transform your fashion brand from concept to reality.

In the tech world, startups are known for their speed and ingenuity. They don't wait for perfection; they launch with an MVP (Minimum Viable Product)—a stripped-down version of their idea designed to test the market and gather feedback. Fashion brands can learn from this approach, embracing innovation, adaptability, and customer-centric design.

In this chapter, I challenge you to think like a tech innovator. Be agile, embrace feedback, and let your MVP be the foundation of your brand's growth. The journey starts now.

Sara Beckman, a faculty member at UC Berkeley's Haas School of Business, is recognised for her work in design thinking, product development, and innovation processes. She has integrated concepts like the Minimum Viable Product (MVP) into her new product development and design thinking teachings. While her direct focus has been on fostering problem-solving skills through practical and iterative methodologies, she also emphasises the importance of observing and understanding customer needs, rapid prototyping, and refining solutions based on continuous feedback.

In her courses, such as *Managing the New product Development Process* and *Problem Finding and Problem-Solving*, Beckman emphasises five steps in the innovation cycle: **Understand, Observe, Synthesise, Realise, and experiment.** These steps align closely with the iterative and agile principles behind the MVP approach, which emphasises customer-centricity and quick feedback loops.

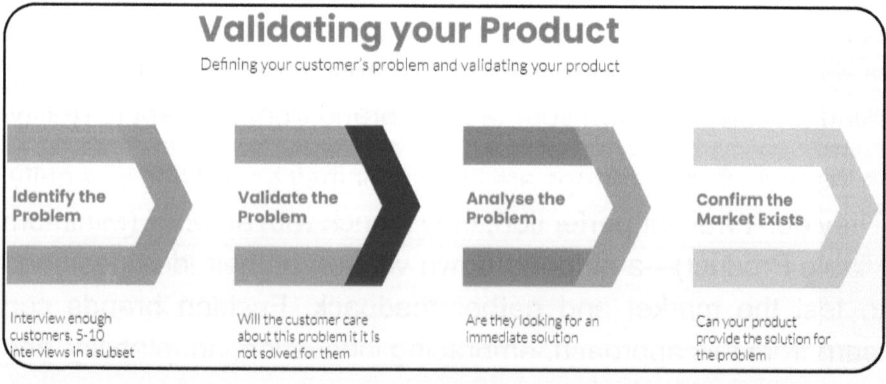

Her work often incorporates cross-disciplinary tools, such as Alexander Osterwalder's *Business Model Canvas*, which helps students visualise and iterate on business ideas effectively.

Understand: Define the problem, challenge, or opportunity. Then, learn as much as possible from subject matter experts and other sources about what is already known in that space.

Observe: Collect first-hand information from customers, users, and other stakeholders by asking open-ended questions, watching people and processes, and engaging them in co-creation activities.

Synthesise (and Analyse): Identify patterns and anomalies in the data gathered and generate insights to create new concepts.

Realise: Generate a large set of alternative solutions, then narrow that down to a few.

Experiment: Embody the selected solutions in artefacts, gather feedback from a variety of stakeholders, and iteratively refine the solutions.

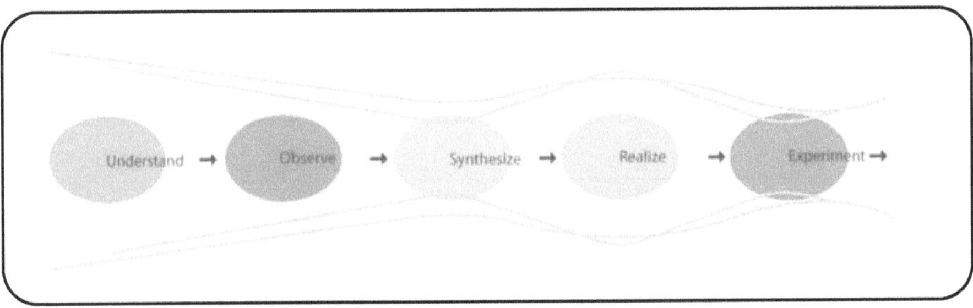

In today's fast-paced fashion world, thinking like a tech startup can set your brand apart. Tech startups thrive on agility, innovation, and customer feedback—increasingly vital qualities in the fashion industry.

1. **Begin with the MVP (Minimum Viable Product):** Like a tech company tests its prototype app with basic features, your first product line should focus on solving a specific customer need. Think of Everlane's debut: a single, high-quality t-shirt emphasising pricing transparency. Everlane debuted as an e-commerce-only brand, avoiding physical stores to focus on streamlined operations and lower overhead costs. The first products were minimalist, high-quality T-shirts priced at $15, significantly cheaper than comparable items at luxury brands. The DTC model allowed Everlane to control branding, storytelling, and customer experience while passing cost savings to consumers. Everlane faced competition from fast-fashion giants like Zara and H&M, which could produce cheaper items more quickly. However, Everlane distinguished itself by emphasising ethical practices and durability.

The MVP, or Minimum Viable Product, is a foundational concept borrowed from the tech world. However, its principles are profoundly practical in the fashion and retail industries. An MVP is a streamlined version of your product that focuses on the core features necessary to meet early adopters' needs. It's about testing the waters before diving in, gathering feedback, refining your product, and minimising risk.

Why Start with an MVP?

1. **Cost-Effectiveness:** Launching a full product line is expensive. By starting with an MVP, you conserve resources while identifying what works.
2. **Faster Time to Market:** An MVP lets you introduce your product quickly, gaining customer feedback before competitors respond. The proverb "fail fast" has recently been used in the startup world, where you want to try

your ideas and move on if they don't work. Implement the learnings in a new startup.

3. **Validated Learning:** Testing your MVP will help you understand your target audience's preferences, reducing the risk of launching a product no one wants. This will be very important when fine-tuning the product or offerings.
4. **Start Lean, Think Big:** Building a massive product line isn't necessary. Focus on one product that represents your vision. Like Allbirds began with a single wool sneaker, simplicity can make waves. Many new brands begin by focusing on a single product, dedicating their efforts to making it successful before expanding their portfolio.

In Eric Ries's *the Lean Startup*, the **Minimum Viable Product (MVP)** is a central concept in building businesses and products. An MVP is the simplest product version that allows a team to collect the maximum amount of validated learning about customers with the least effort. This process underscores the importance of failing fast and learning early, ensuring businesses only invest further in ideas with proven demand.

The goal is not to sell a fully polished product but to **test hypotheses** and **validate customer needs and preferences assumptions**. MVPs prioritise **speed and learning** over perfection.

1. **Building the MVP**
   - Focus on developing only the **core functionalities** needed to solve a problem or test a hypothesis. If you try too many functionalities, analysing the feedback will be challenging.
   - Avoid over-engineering or spending excessive time on features that might not matter to customers. Founders often focus on perfecting and enhancing their products, which can lead to delays in the launch. This approach

prolongs the timeline and increases costs in terms of time and resources.

2. **Validated Learning**

    - MVPs generate data on whether a product idea is viable, ensuring decisions are grounded in evidence rather than assumptions.
    - For example, companies can analyse user interactions with MVPs to determine whether their solution addresses a real customer problem.

Some Examples that the author mentioned are

- **Dropbox:** Before developing the complete product, the team created a simple explainer video to showcase the concept. The overwhelming interest and sign-ups validated the idea.
- **Zappos:** Founder Nick Swinmurn tested the idea of an online shoe store by posting pictures of shoes from local stores. When customers made purchases, he bought the shoes and shipped them himself, validating demand for the concept.

3. **Iterative Process**

    - After launching the MVP, teams iterate based on customer feedback to improve the product incrementally.
    - This ensures that time and resources are directed towards what truly matters to customers.

4. **The "Build-Measure-Learn" Feedback Loop**

    - The MVP is part of a continuous cycle: **Build** a product, **Measure** customer responses, and **Learn** from the results to refine the product.

5. **Test and Learn:** Releasing an MVP lets you listen to customers, refine your product, and iterate quickly. This

feedback loop is the secret to staying relevant in a dynamic market.

Test Early and Frequently

- Testing begins with hypotheses about the product, market, or customer needs.
- Entrepreneurs design experiments—often using MVPs (Minimum Viable Products)—to validate these assumptions as quickly and cheaply as possible.
- The purpose is to uncover whether a business idea aligns with market demand before scaling up or investing heavily.

Run Based on Feedback

- Once tests yield results, teams decide whether to **pivot** (change direction) or **persevere** (refine the idea).
- Running involves executing strategies or product iterations informed by the collected data.

'If we're building something that nobody wants, it doesn't matter if we're doing it on time and budget.' – Eric Ries.

Testing ensures alignment with customer needs, allowing teams to move in the right direction.

6. **Data is Your Compass:** Tech startups leverage analytics to guide decisions. Similarly, understanding customer preferences through surveys, pre-orders, or small product launches can shape your brand's future.

Think of your MVP as the seed of a giant tree. It starts small, but it can grow into something magnificent with nurturing and attention.

Mistakes aren't failures – they're the soil where your brand's roots deepen.

According to CB Insights, 35% of startups fail because there's no market need for their product. Testing an MVP can help you avoid this pitfall.

Over 80% of Fortune 500 companies have adopted the Lean Startup methodology, which emphasises MVPs.

> *"The fastest way to succeed is to fail fast and learn faster." – Eric Ries.*

Business Model Canvas

A Business Model Canvas (BMC) is a single-page template that outlines a business's goals and objectives. As a strategic management tool, a BMC can help business owners and other stakeholders develop new business models or evaluate existing ones.

Alexander Osterwalder and Yves Pigneur co-created the Business Model Canvas (BMC) in 2005. At the time, it was revolutionary, offering a simplified, visual alternative to the traditional business plan. The BMC led to the creation of other canvases, such as the Lean Canvas Model, which is explicitly used to validate a business idea, and the Value Proposition Canvas, which helps identify whether a product or service meets customers' needs.

BUSINESS MODEL CANVAS

KEY PARTNERS	KEY ACTIVITIES / KEY RESOURCES	VALUE PROPOSITIONS	CUSTOMER RELATIONSHIP / CHANNELS	CUSTOMER SEGMENTS
COST STRUCTURE		REVENUE STREAM		

The Business Model Canvas consists of nine building blocks, each represented by a rectangle.

1. **Key partners:** A business's key partnerships include stakeholders, joint ventures, and strategic alliances that will help it achieve its objectives. This is also where to consider suppliers.
2. **Key activities:** A business's key activities are all the tasks and responsibilities necessary to make the business model work, including its revenue streams. These include production tasks, marketing or networking activities, and problem-solving.
3. **Key resources:** Your key resources are the primary assets you will need to complete your key activities. This could include employees, finances, equipment, or intellectual property.
4. **Value proposition:** A business's value proposition is its unique offering or solution to its customers. It might be a new product or service customers can't get anywhere else or an improved version of an existing product or service.
5. **Customer relationships:** This building block involves defining the customer's relationship to the business and

examining the customer experience. Some companies require personal assistance, while others are self-service.

6. **Customer segments:** This involves defining the customer base or the types of people (or businesses) the company will target. The more specific the target customer demographics, the easier it is to understand the customer journey and meet customer needs. Multiple customer types are possible, and it's vital to list them and rank them by importance.
7. **Channels:** Channels are how businesses communicate with and market to their customers. This includes distribution channels for getting goods or services to customers. Channels can be owned by the industry, such as a company website or storefront, by partners or third parties, such as retailers or partners who stock the business's product, or through word-of-mouth marketing.
8. **Cost structure:** The cost structure defines all the business's costs during operation, including variable and fixed costs. Consider the costs of starting a new business and the daily costs of maintaining an existing business.
9. **Revenue streams:** A company's revenue streams are how the business makes money. These could be single transactions, like selling assets, or recurring sales, such as monthly subscription fees.

Fashion and Retail Industry Examples

1. **Fabindia**

   - **MVP Approach:** When Fabindia began in 1960, it focused on a single product category: handwoven textiles. These products highlighted the richness of Indian craftsmanship.
   - **Outcome:** By perfecting its supply chain and understanding the demand for sustainable, handmade

products, FabIndia expanded into apparel, home decor, and organic foods while staying true to its roots.

- **Key Insight:** Their MVP allowed them to validate the market's interest in ethically sourced, artisan products before diversifying.

---

2. **Biba**

- **MVP Approach:** Biba's initial offering in the 1980s was a small line of salwar kameez dupatta sets that appealed to middle-class Indian women looking for ready-made ethnic wear.
- **Outcome:** The success of this simple, well-priced MVP laid the foundation for Biba's growth into a leader in women's ethnic wear, offering a wide range of styles across India.
- **Key Insight:** Focusing on a specific problem, affordable, stylish ethnic wear—helped Biba build brand loyalty early on.

---

3. **Nykaa Fashion**

- **MVP Approach:** Nykaa started as a beauty e-commerce platform with a curated selection of products but expanded into Nykaa Fashion by testing limited categories of clothing, accessories, and footwear before scaling.
- **Outcome:** The platform is now a key player in the Indian fashion retail space, housing premium and homegrown brands.
- **Key Insight:** Nykaa's focus on data-driven decision-making and MVP testing allowed it to enter the fashion retail seamlessly.

---

4. **The Loom**
    - **MVP Approach:** The Loom started by offering a small collection of handwoven sarees and dupattas online, appealing to customers who valued sustainable fashion and Indian artistry.
    - **Outcome:** The Loom grew into a trusted name for curated, handcrafted clothing and accessories by focusing on quality and storytelling.
    - **Key Insight:** A limited but well-curated MVP helped them gauge demand for artisanal products without overextending.

---

5. **Raw Mango**
    - **MVP Approach:** Sanjay Garg's Raw Mango began with a limited collection of handwoven sarees that celebrated Indian textiles in a contemporary context.
    - **Outcome:** Its minimalist approach to traditional wear resonated with a modern audience, allowing it to grow into a global brand.
    - **Key Insight:** Starting with a niche product helped Raw Mango craft a unique identity and establish a loyal customer base.

Your MVP is not just a product – it's a conversation with your customers. By starting lean and learning quickly, you create a brand that evolves with your audience.

As Reid Hoffman, co-founder of LinkedIn, once said: *"If you are not embarrassed by the first version of your product, you've launched too late."*

Listen to Your Customers

Real-time feedback through social media, reviews, and surveys can guide swift changes.

Building Speed and Adaptability Through Feedback

In today's fast-paced fashion industry, listening to your customers isn't just an added value—it's the core of staying relevant and agile. Customers are your brand's lifeline, providing insights that can shape product development, marketing, and even business strategy. **According to a PwC study, brands that incorporate customer feedback into their decision-making processes are 60% more likely to achieve faster growth.**[9]

Why Listening Matters

Fashion trends evolve rapidly, and customer preferences can shift in the blink of an eye. Proactively seeking feedback can address pain points, improve your offerings, and build loyalty. Listening also humanises your brand, making customers feel valued and connected.

Examples of Feedback Integration

1. **H&M's Conscious Collection:** H&M collects customer feedback on sustainability concerns through online surveys and in-store feedback forms. Their Conscious Collection directly responded to the growing demand for eco-friendly options, helping the brand stay ahead in the sustainable fashion market.
2. **Nykaa Fashion (India):** Nykaa actively engages with its customer base through social media polls and reviews. This real-time feedback loop helps them tweak product

9 https://www.pwc.de/de/consulting/pwc-consumer-intelligence-series-customer-experience.pdf?utm_source=chatgpt.com

assortments and launch targeted campaigns like their festive wear collections, resonating with Indian customers.

3. **Levi's Tailor Shops:** Levi's listens to its audience by offering customisable jeans in-store, based on feedback that customers wanted unique and personalised items.

Steps to Build a Feedback System

1. **Social Listening:** Use tools like Sprout Social or Hootsuite to monitor customer mentions, reviews, and complaints on platforms like Instagram or Twitter.
2. **Surveys:** Conduct regular surveys to understand customer satisfaction. For example, "Would you recommend this product to a friend?" helps gauge loyalty (Net Promoter Score).
3. **Focus Groups:** Engage small groups to discuss specific products, especially when entering new markets.
4. **AI-Powered Insights:** Utilise tools like Google Analytics and machine learning to track buying patterns and understand customer needs.

Statistics That Prove the Power of Listening

- 76% of consumers expect brands to understand their needs and preferences (Salesforce).
- 41% of customers stop buying from brands that fail to personalise their experience (Accenture).

Zivame, an Indian lingerie retailer, realised customers were uncomfortable shopping in physical stores due to privacy concerns. They expanded their online services by analysing feedback, conducting surveys, and introducing discreet packaging. This pivot increased their customer retention by 30%.

Zivame - Redefining Lingerie Retail in India

Zivame, a pioneering Indian lingerie retailer founded in 2011 by Richa Kar, disrupted the market by addressing a critical cultural and societal challenge: the discomfort Indian women faced while shopping for intimate wear in traditional brick-and-mortar stores. By leveraging customer insights, Zivame transformed the lingerie shopping experience, offering solutions that prioritised privacy, convenience, and inclusivity.[10]

The Challenge

In India, lingerie shopping was traditionally an awkward experience for women. Societal taboos, male-dominated staff in stores, and a lack of privacy created an environment where women often avoided discussing their actual needs or preferences.

Key Pain Points Identified

1. Lack of privacy in physical retail environments.
2. Limited size and style options in traditional stores.
3. Reluctance to seek advice or discuss preferences with sales staff.
4. A cultural stigma attached to open conversations about lingerie.

---

10 **Meet Richa Kar, founder of India's largest online lingerie shop Zivame, acquired by Mukesh Ambani, who amassed Rs 749 crores... Zivame was aquired by Reliance retail in 2020**
Written by FE Lifestyle
Updated: July 26, 2023, 14:16 IST

Customer Feedback That Drove Change

Zivame conducted surveys and focus groups and gathered feedback through online interactions. Their research highlighted:

- Over 70% of women felt uncomfortable shopping for lingerie in physical stores.
- Many women were unaware of their correct size and avoided professional fittings.
- There was a strong demand for discreet and personalised shopping experiences.

The Solution

Zivame adopted a two-pronged strategy: building an online-first platform and enhancing the in-store experience with customer-centric innovations.

1. **Online Store**
    - Launched a comprehensive e-commerce platform where women could discreetly browse, choose, and purchase lingerie.
    - Introduced features like size calculators and fit assistants to help customers find the perfect product.
    - Offering discreet packaging to address privacy concerns.
2. **Physical Retail Redefined**
    - Rolled out Zivame Studios, experiential stores designed to ensure privacy and comfort.
    - Created trial rooms with personalised fittings and trained female staff to assist customers.
    - Built a welcoming environment, including comfortable seating areas, educational materials, and size charts.

3. **Community Building**

   - Focused on education and empowerment through blogs, workshops, and campaigns like #FitForAll, emphasising body positivity and size inclusivity.

Results and Impact

Zivame's innovations redefined lingerie shopping in India, leading to significant brand loyalty and market share growth.

Key Metrics

- **30% increase in customer retention** after launching their discreet packaging and improved fitting tools.
- An estimated **10 million customers** will be served by 2023, with a significant portion being first-time buyers.
- Physical stores reported a **40% increase in footfall** after implementing privacy-driven changes.

Lessons from sZivame's Success

1. **Listening to Customers**: By understanding the cultural and emotional barriers Indian women faced, Zivame created solutions that directly addressed these pain points.
2. **Omnichannel Approach**: The brand's ability to balance a strong online presence with reimagined physical stores helped it cater to diverse customer preferences.
3. **Empowerment through Education**: Zivame's focus on educating customers about proper sizing and lingerie care fostered trust and brand loyalty.

Conclusion

Zivame's journey is a testament to the power of customer-centric innovation. By breaking cultural taboos and addressing deeply ingrained societal challenges, Zivame built a successful brand and empowered millions of Indian women. Their story highlights the importance of empathy and adaptability in creating a brand that resonates with its audience. Richa Kar once said, "Zivame is not just a lingerie brand—it's a movement to help women feel confident and comfortable in their skin."

Listening to your customers is about responding to complaints and co-creating your brand's future. As Tony Robbins says, "Successful people ask better questions, and as a result, they get better answers." Engaging with your customers ensures your brand evolves with their needs, staying fast and adaptable in a competitive market.

Final Thought

Think of your fashion brand as a surfer riding waves. The ocean (the market) is unpredictable, but with the right board (processes) and sharp reflexes (adaptability), you can catch every wave that comes your way. As Benjamin Franklin aptly said, "When you're finished changing, you're finished."

Embracing speed and adaptability isn't just about staying competitive; it's about creating a brand that thrives amidst constant change.

Ask yourself:

- What's the simplest version of your product that solves a real problem?
- How can you test your concept with minimal resources?
- Write down your answers to create a lean product roadmap.

Think of your brand as a newborn bird learning to fly. The MVP is its first leap – a little rough, maybe uncertain, but full of potential. With each attempt, it grows stronger.

> *"Move fast and break things." – Mark Zuckerberg.*

Key takeaways: From Idea to MVP - Building the Foundation:

Think Like a Tech Startup

- Adopt agility and innovation as foundational principles.
- Focus on creating a **Minimum Viable Product (MVP)** to quickly test and validate ideas before investing heavily.

Why Start with an MVP?

1. **Cost-Effectiveness**: Launching a full product line is expensive; MVPs help conserve resources.
2. **Faster Time to Market**: MVPs enable quick launches and allow brands to iterate based on honest customer feedback.
3. **Validated Learning**: Testing an MVP helps brands refine products based on evidence rather than assumptions.

4. **Start Lean, Think Big**: Begin with a niche product representing your brand's vision, like Allbirds' wool sneaker or Everlane's transparent pricing model.

Building the MVP

- Focus on solving one core problem with the most straightforward product version.
- Use the **Build-Measure-Learn** feedback loop to iterate and improve.
- Avoid over-engineering; prioritise speed and responsiveness over perfection.

Feedback and Iteration

- Customer feedback is critical for refining and aligning your product with market needs.
- Use tools like surveys, pre-orders, and small product launches to understand customer preferences.
- Successful brands like Dropbox, Zappos, and Everlane used MVPs to validate their ideas and build strong customer bases.

Leverage the Business Model Canvas (BMC)

- Use tools like Alexander Osterwalder's **BMC** to map key business elements, such as customer segments, value propositions, revenue streams, etc.
- Refine your approach by identifying gaps and iterating on business strategies effectively.

The Power of Feedback

- **Listen Actively**: Use social media polls, surveys, and focus groups to engage with customers.
- **Be Adaptable**: Stay agile by iterating based on customer insights and market trends.

An MVP is more than a product; it's a conversation with your customers. Starting small and iterating quickly sets a solid foundation for a brand that grows, evolves, and resonates deeply with its audience.

Chapter 4

"Threads of Connection: Crafting a Brand Story That Resonates"

"Authenticity, Emotion, and Impact in Fashion Storytelling"

"People will forget what you said and did but never forget how you made them feel." – Maya Angelou.

Brand Storytelling

How to Shape a Compelling Brand Narrative

In a crowded marketplace, a well-crafted brand story is your secret weapon. Beyond logos and catchy slogans, storytelling humanises your brand and forges emotional connections with your audience. For fashion brands, this means weaving a narrative that resonates with their target customers' values, dreams, and aspirations.

Storytelling Matters: People don't just buy products – they buy the story behind them. What story will your brand tell?

Storytelling is the soul of your brand. A compelling narrative sets you apart in a saturated fashion market where every brand offers similar products. People don't just buy clothes; they purchase the emotions, experiences, and values your brand represents.

The Power of a Story

Stories have the power to connect emotionally with customers.

Brands with strong narratives see a **22% higher customer loyalty** (Harvard Business Review)[11]

11 **"Want More Loyal Customers? Offer a community, Not Rewards"** - This article discusses how true loyalty comes from a sense of identity and belonging rather than just rewards.

Harvard Business Review frequently publishes insights on branding and customer loyalty. Its research often highlights the importance of narrative in building strong emotional connections with consumers, which can directly impact loyalty and trust.

A Nielsen study shows that **63% of consumers remember brands better with stories than those with just facts or advertisements**[12]

Nielsen's findings suggest that storytelling in marketing significantly enhances brand recall. This is linked to the idea that consumers engage more deeply with brands providing relatable, emotional, or purpose-driven content. The report also states personalised and contextualised content, such as stories, significantly improves purchasing likelihood. You can explore detailed consumer insights from Nielsen's reports at Nielsen's official site or look at their consumer research reports.

Your brand story should answer the following:

Who are you? Share your origin. Why did you start the brand?

- **Ritu Kumar** emphasises her beginnings as a revivalist of traditional Indian craftsmanship, now a globally recognised designer.

What Problem are you solving? Focus on how your products address customer pain points.

- **Nicobar** focuses on sustainability and minimalism, addressing the desire for eco-friendly luxury.

  Why should customers care? Highlight your values, such as inclusivity or sustainability, and how they align with your audience.

---

12 Nielsen report titled **"Brand Storytelling in 2024: The Latest Statistics and Trends"**

- A McKinsey study found that **45% of Gen Z shoppers are more likely to support brands that tell authentic stories about their products**[13]
- Highlight the positive impact of your brand, such as jobs created, or eco-friendly materials used.

What Makes a Brand Story Compelling?

The four essential factors that make a compelling brand story are

1. Authenticity
2. Relatability
3. Emotional impact
4. Consistency

Authenticity: Your story must reflect your brand's mission, vision, and values.

Authenticity is the cornerstone of impactful brand storytelling. It bridges the gap between a brand and its audience by creating trust and emotional connections. Authenticity means aligning your narrative with your actions, values, and customer experiences for fashion brands.

Why Authenticity Matters

Studies reveal that **86% of consumers prioritise authenticity when deciding which brands to support** (Stackla, 2021)[14]. This is especially critical in the fashion industry, where transparency

---

13 McKinsey study titled **"The Rise of the Inclusive Consumer"**.

14 Stackla report titled **"Post-Pandemic Shifts in Consumer Shopping Habits: Authenticity, Personalisation and the Power of UGC"** published in August 2021. The report highlights that **86% of Gen Z and 81% of Millennial shoppers** are more likely to buy from e-Commerce sites that display user-generated content (UGC) visuals

around sustainability, sourcing, and labour practices is increasingly scrutinised.

Authentic stories tap into human emotions, creating memorable experiences. Stories about ethical craftsmanship or community support resonate deeply with customers.

Relatability: Highlight elements that connect with your audience's lifestyle or challenges.

Relatability is creating stories that resonate deeply with your target audience by reflecting their emotions, aspirations, and values. For fashion brands, this means understanding their audience so well that their narrative feels about them, not just their product.

Why Relatability Matters

Emotional Connection: Brands that tell relatable stories create lasting emotional bonds. According to a **Harvard Business Review study**, emotionally connected customers are **52% more valuable**[15] to a brand than satisfied but unengaged customers.

Increased Engagement: Nielsen research[16] shows **63% of consumers prefer brands whose stories align with their beliefs or lifestyles.**

Brand Advocacy: Customers who see themselves in a brand's story are more likely to recommend it to others.

Emotional Impact: Use narratives that evoke feelings, whether it's nostalgia, aspiration, or hope.

---

15 Harvard Business Review article titled **"An Emotional Connection Matters More than Customer Satisfaction"** by Alan Zorfas and Daniel Leemon

16 Nielsen report titled **"Era of Alignment"** from their 2022 Annual Marketing Report

Emotions are the foundation of compelling brand narratives. Stories that evoke joy, hope, nostalgia, or even vulnerability connect with audiences on a deeper level, making the brand memorable and fostering loyalty. This emotional resonance is particularly vital for fashion brands, as fashion is an inherently personal expression of identity.

Why Emotional Impact Matters

Stronger Brand Recall: A study by **IPA DataBank** found that emotionally charged campaigns are **31% more effective** at driving brand value than campaigns focused purely on rational content.[17]

Increased Purchase Intent: Nielsen data shows that ads with emotional content generate a **23% increase in sales** compared to neutral campaigns.

Enhanced Loyalty: Customers are more likely to remain loyal to brands that make them feel understood and valued.

Consistency: Ensure every touchpoint (social media, packaging, website) aligns with the story.

Consistency in storytelling is the foundation of a recognisable and trustworthy brand identity. It ensures that every interaction, message, and visual reflects the same core values, tone, and mission, reinforcing a brand's position in consumers' minds.

---

17 study by Les Binet and Peter Field titled **"The Long and the Short of It"**. This book analyses the IPA Databank of 996 campaigns entered into the IPA Effectiveness Awards between 1980 and 20101. One of the key findings is that **emotional campaigns are almost twice as likely to result in top-box profit growth** over the long-term compared to rational campaigns

Why Consistency Matters

1. **Builds Trust**: A **Lucidpress survey** found that consistent brand presentation increases revenue by **33%** on average, as customers are more likely to trust brands that deliver a unified experience.
2. **Enhances Recognition**: A report by **Forbes Insights** highlights that **90% of consumers expect consistent interactions across all platforms** and are more likely to recall brands with cohesive messaging.
3. **Fosters' Emotional Connection**: A consistent narrative reassures consumers that the brand stays faithful to its promises, deepening loyalty over time.

Examples of Consistent Brand Storytelling

1. **H&M**: Globally, H&M ensures consistency by tying all campaigns to its core mission of "fashion and quality at the best price in a sustainable way." This theme extends from advertisements to in-store experiences, ensuring sustainability remains central.
2. **Manish Malhotra (India)**: This luxury designer maintains a consistent narrative of glamour, Indian heritage, and luxury across runway shows, social media, and retail spaces.
3. **Zara**: Known for "fast-fashion," Zara maintains consistency in storytelling by focusing on immediacy and trend alignment across its global platforms. Customers know they'll find the latest trends every time they visit Zara.

Indian Fashion Industry Examples

1. **FabIndia**
   - **The Story:** FabIndia connects its brand to India's rich artisan heritage. Its story revolves around sustainability and empowering rural artisans.
   - **Impact:** Customers feel that purchasing each garment contributes to a larger purpose—preserving heritage and supporting artisans.
   - **Lesson:** Align your brand story with social impact to create loyalty.
2. **Raw Mango**
   - **The Story:** Raw Mango blends traditional Indian crafts with modern aesthetics. Its storytelling emphasises cultural revival through handloom fabrics in contemporary designs.
   - **Impact:** They've built a niche audience that values heritage and exclusivity.
   - **Lesson:** Focusing on cultural storytelling can create a powerful niche.
3. **Nykaa Fashion**
   - **The Story:** Nykaa narrates a journey of empowerment, offering fashion as a tool for self-expression.
   - **Impact:** The relatable, aspirational narrative resonates with young, style-conscious Indians.
   - **Lesson:** Personalisation in storytelling enhances audience engagement.

Global Statistics Supporting Brand Storytelling

- **92% of consumers** want brands to create ads that feel like a story (Forbes).[18]
- **55% of consumers** are more likely to buy from a brand with a relatable tale (Harvard Business Review).[19]
- **50% of Gen Z and Millennials** prefer brands with a purpose-driven narrative (Deloitte).[20]

How to Build a Great Brand Narrative

1. **The Beginning – Origin Story:**
2. Share why you started your brand. Was it a gap in the market, a personal journey, or a passion project?
    - Example: Highlight how your love for sustainable materials inspired your collection.
3. **The Middle – Journey and Growth**
4. Narrate struggles, milestones, and lessons that shaped your brand's journey.
    - Example: Share how you adapted during the pandemic to stay relevant.
5. **The Future – Aspiration**
6. Discuss where your brand is heading and how your audience can be part of the journey.

---

18 **"Brand Storytelling in 2024: The Latest Statistics and Trends"** on **The Brand Shop BW Blog**

19 **"The Power of Storytelling in Marketing"** on the Harvard Business Review website.

20 Deloitte website or in the Forbes article titled **"Gen Zs and Millennials Seek Purpose And Progress In A Changing World: Insights From Deloitte's 2024 Gen Z and Millennial Survey"**

- Example: Emphasise a vision for sustainability, inclusivity, or innovation.

As the fashion industry evolves, key trends are reshaping consumer behaviour and market dynamics: Revolutionising product Discovery Through AI. Consumers today face overwhelming choices, hindering their engagement and conversion with fashion brands. Generative AI is emerging as a transformative solution, enabling tailored product curation through advanced content and search capabilities. In the future, half of fashion executives expect AI-driven discovery to be a pivotal innovation, signalling a shift towards hyper-personalised shopping experiences. Disruptive players in the sportswear segment are gaining ground. They are projected to account for over half of the sector's economic profits. Success will hinge on creating innovative products, leveraging influential ambassadors, and crafting compelling brand narratives through strategic channels.

One of the forwards on social media was interesting. It says as follows,

Apple sells innovation, not phones.

Rolex sells status, not watches

Lego sells Creativity, not toys

Nike sells motivation, not shoes

Coca-Cola sells happiness, not drinks, and

Tesla sells the future, not cars. Success is about selling emotions, not products.

---

1. What is the unique story behind your brand?
2. How does your story connect emotionally with your audience?
3. Can your story inspire trust and loyalty in customers?

Key Takeaways from the Chapter:

1. **Storytelling as a Differentiator**
    - In a crowded market, a well-crafted brand story is a powerful tool for humanising your brand, resonating with your audience, and setting you apart from competitors.
    - Consumers don't just buy products – they buy the emotions, values, and experiences your brand represents.
2. **The Power of Emotional Connections**
    - Emotional narratives foster trust, loyalty, and brand recall.
    - Statistics show that brands with strong storytelling see significantly higher customer loyalty and purchase intent.
3. **Elements of a Compelling Brand Story**
    - Authenticity: Align your story with your brand's mission, vision, and values.
    - Relatability: Highlight elements that resonate with your audience's lifestyle, challenges, or aspirations.
    - Emotional Impact: Craft narratives that evoke joy, hope, nostalgia, or vulnerability.
    - Consistency: Ensure your story is reflected across all touchpoints, from social media to packaging.

4. **Building Your Brand Narrative**
   - Origin Story: Share why you started your brand—your motivation, challenges, and inspirations.
   - Journey and Growth: Narrate milestones, struggles, and adaptations that shaped your brand's identity.
   - Future Aspirations: Describe your brand's future direction and how customers can participate.

5. **Storytelling in Action**
   - Authentic storytelling can highlight positive impacts such as sustainability or community support, fostering deeper emotional connections.
   - Align your narrative with the experiences and aspirations of your target audience to inspire trust and loyalty.

6. **Inspirational Perspective**
   - Leading brands sell emotions, not just products (e.g., Nike sells motivation, Coca-Cola sells happiness, and Tesla sells the future).

7. **Self-Reflection Questions for Your Brand**
   - What is the unique story behind your brand?
   - How does your story emotionally connect with your audience?
   - Can your story inspire trust and long-term loyalty in customers?

Compelling storytelling is not just a marketing strategy but the soul of a brand. It can create lasting relationships and drive meaningful connections with customers.

Part Two

PRODUCT AND LAUNCH

Chapter 5

Developing a Product Strategy

"To accomplish great things, we must not only act but also dream; not only plan but also believe." – Anatole France.

In the crowded world of fashion and retail, standing out is no longer an option—it's a necessity. Product positioning is the art of crafting a distinct identity for your brand in the minds of your target audience. It's about answering a simple yet profound question: *Why should customers choose your product over someone else's?*

Imagine walking into a bustling marketplace filled with identical stalls. Each one calls out, offering similar wares at similar prices. Now, picture one stall that tells a different story that resonates with your values, identity, and desires. That's the power of product positioning: transforming your brand into a beacon of relatability, trust, and value.

In today's fast-paced apparel industry, where trends fade as quickly as they emerge, positioning is the foundation for long-term success. It's not just about selling clothes; it's about selling meaning, emotion, and connection. For example, the luxury brand Gucci symbolises unapologetic individuality and opulence, while Patagonia's eco-conscious positioning speaks to consumers who prioritise sustainability.

Fashion brands like Zara, Uniqlo, and Levi's have mastered the art of positioning and strategically tailoring their identity to resonate with distinct customer bases. This chapter will unravel how to leverage product positioning to create a compelling narrative, differentiate from competitors, and ultimately dominate your niche market.

As you embark on this journey, remember that your brand's position isn't just about where it stands on a shelf – it's about where it lives in your customers' hearts and minds. That's where loyalty begins.

Product Positioning and Differentiation

Understanding Product Positioning

Product positioning is the strategic process of defining how a product fits into the market landscape and how customers perceive it compared to competitors. In the fast-paced apparel and retail industry, clear and compelling positioning is critical to capturing attention in an oversaturated market.

For apparel brands, positioning goes beyond style and price—intertwining with identity, values, and lifestyle. For example, H&M positions itself as a fast-fashion leader offering affordable runway trends, while Patagonia markets its products as environmentally sustainable, appealing to conscious consumers. Decathlon offers products only related to sports and outdoor travel gear, such as camping, hiking, and mountaineering, etc.

The Importance of Differentiation

Differentiation is how a brand sets itself apart by offering unique value. In the apparel industry, where trends quickly become commodities, differentiation is a survival tool. The right strategy can transform a basic t-shirt into a symbol of luxury, sustainability, or cultural identity.

In a world where fashion brands emerge daily, blending into the crowd is the quickest way to fail. Differentiation is not just a strategy; it's the lifeline of any successful brand. It answers the pivotal question: *What makes your brand unique?* And creates an identity that resonates deeply with your target audience.

Successful differentiation goes beyond products—crafting a distinct narrative, delivering value, and forging an emotional connection. Consider Nike, a brand synonymous with innovation and empowerment. It stands out for its products and ethos: inspiring athletes to “Just Do It.” Similarly, India's FabIndia has carved a niche by combining traditional craftsmanship with contemporary design, creating an identity rooted in culture and authenticity.

New fashion industry entrepreneurs must embrace differentiation as a mindset rather than a task. Your brand should offer something competitors cannot replicate—whether through innovative materials, exceptional customer experiences, or deeply personalised marketing. Remember, differentiation doesn't always mean being the best; it's about being memorable and relevant to your audience.

For budding entrepreneurs, differentiation is about asking hard questions: *What gap does my product fill? What emotional need does it address? How can my brand consistently delight customers?* Answering these questions sets the stage for building a brand that isn't just seen—it's remembered.

Differentiation is your ticket to cutting through the noise, capturing hearts, and building a legacy. After all, in a sea of sameness, the bold and unique always rise above.

Best Practices for Differentiation in Apparel

1. Value-Based Differentiation: Value-based differentiation focuses on creating unique value for the customer by offering products that go beyond price competition. This could mean emphasising sustainability, ethical sourcing, or multifunctionality in the apparel industry. The goal is to align the brand's offerings with the values and priorities of its target customers, fostering loyalty and emotional connection.
    - Patagonia promotes environmental responsibility by using recycled materials, attracting eco-conscious customers.
2. Niche Focus: Niche focus involves tailoring products and marketing strategies to serve a particular market segment. In apparel, this could be a specific lifestyle, cultural identity, or functional need, such as activewear for yoga enthusiasts or clothing for petite sizes. By deeply understanding and addressing the needs of this smaller audience, brands can create strong customer loyalty and reduce competition.
    - Decathlon focuses on sports apparel and equipment. It designs, develops, and offers only specific products for sports and outdoor activities.
    - Targeting specific demographics or lifestyles creates a loyal customer base.
3. Quality and Craftsmanship: Quality and craftsmanship differentiation emphasises superior materials, attention to detail, and exceptional production standards. This could mean using premium fabrics, employing skilled artisans, or ensuring durability and fit in apparel. Customers are willing to pay a premium for clothing that reflects meticulous care and quality, which also helps establish a brand's reputation.

   - Levi's positions itself with the durability and authenticity of its denim products.

4. Innovative Design: Innovative design leverages creativity and forward-thinking approaches to create unique, trendsetting products. This could include functional innovations (e.g., moisture-wicking fabrics), aesthetic originality (e.g., bold patterns or unique silhouettes), or combining technology with fashion (e.g., bright clothing). Brands that differentiate through innovation often become leaders and trendsetters in their market segment.

   - Uniqlo differentiates itself with its HeatTech fabric, which appeals to functionality-driven customers.

Product Strategy in Apparel and Retail

Effective product strategies align with customer needs, market trends, and brand identity. Key components include:

A Customer-Centric Approach is a business strategy that prioritises the customer's needs, preferences, and experiences at every stage of the buying journey. It involves designing products, services, and interactions around the customer to deliver value, build trust, and foster long-term loyalty.

Brands like Zivame tailor their offerings to customer concerns such as comfort and privacy.

Key Principles of a Customer-Centric Approach

Understanding Customer Needs: This principle involves deep insights into customers' preferences, expectations, and pain points. This might mean researching market trends, analysing purchasing behaviour, or conducting focus groups in apparel.

The goal is to design products and experiences that effectively address these needs, fostering loyalty and satisfaction.

Personalisation: Personalisation of tailors' products, services, and interactions to each customer's preferences. For example, it could include offering customised fits, style recommendations based on past purchases, or exclusive collections for loyal customers in the apparel industry. Personalisation enhances the customer experience by making it more relevant and meaningful.

Empathy and Engagement: Empathy means understanding and addressing customers' emotional and practical needs, while engagement involves building meaningful relationships through regular and genuine interactions. In apparel, this could mean creating relatable marketing campaigns, actively listening to customer concerns, and offering exceptional service.

Feedback-Driven Improvement: This principle emphasises continuously gathering and implementing customer feedback to refine products, services, and processes. An apparel brand could use reviews to improve fit, modify designs based on customer suggestions, or adapt collections to address emerging trends. Feedback ensures the brand evolves in line with customer expectations. A new startup in sports apparel, Cult Sports, sends its collection to many influencers, gets feedback, makes corrections, and launches its collection in the market.

Consistency Across Touchpoints: Consistency ensures that customers have a seamless and unified experience across all interactions with the brand, whether online, in-store, or through customer service. For example, an apparel brand should maintain the same quality, branding, and tone across its website, social media, packaging, and retail outlets. This builds trust and reinforces the brand identity.

Case Study: Nike's Product Positioning Mastery

Nike is a global giant in the sportswear industry, but its success isn't solely due to its high-quality products. The brand's true strength lies in its masterful product positioning, which revolves around empowering athletes and embracing innovation. This case study explores how Nike consistently redefines its market position to maintain dominance.

Nike's famous tagline, *"Just Do It,"* is more than a slogan—it encapsulates the brand's ethos. Nike positions itself not merely as a manufacturer of athletic gear but as a catalyst for personal transformation. This message resonates universally, from professional athletes to everyday fitness enthusiasts.

Nike stands out by combining innovative design with emotional storytelling:

- Nike's "Just Do It" campaign aligns the brand with perseverance and achievement.
- Differentiation: Products like self-lacing sneakers and collaborations with cultural icons keep Nike ahead.
- Impact: In 2022, Nike captured a 39% market share globally in the athletic footwear market.[21]

Key Strategies in Nike's Positioning

1. **Emotional Connection:** Nike's campaigns evoke powerful emotions. Ads like *"You Can't Stop Us"* celebrate diversity, perseverance, and overcoming challenges, establishing the brand as a symbol of inspiration.
2. **Product Innovation:** Nike positions itself as a pioneer in cutting-edge technology. Examples include the Flyknit

---

21 report by **RunRepeat** find more details about this statistic in their article titled "Nike Shoes Statistics".

shoes, which blend lightweight comfort with eco-conscious manufacturing, and the self-lacing HyperAdapt sneakers.

3. **Inclusivity:** Nike's campaigns target a diverse audience, including women, children, and differently abled athletes. Initiatives like Nike Pro Hijab highlight the brand's commitment to inclusivity.
4. **Leveraging Athlete Ambassadors:** Nike aligns its products with excellence and aspiration by collaborating with icons like Michael Jordan and Serena Williams. For instance, the Air Jordan line became a cultural phenomenon through strategic positioning.

Lessons for Entrepreneurs

- **Focus on Purpose:** As Nike inspires athletes, entrepreneurs should build brands that inspire their audience.
- **Invest in Innovation:** Differentiate your product with unique features or designs.
- **Tell Stories That Resonate:** Like Nike, connect emotionally with your audience to create lasting loyalty.

Nike's mastery of product positioning demonstrates that it's not just about what you sell but how you make people feel.

Product positioning and differentiation are not just strategies but essential survival tools in the apparel and retail world. Brands that define and communicate their unique value effectively build lasting customer relationships. Whether creating niche appeal, leading with sustainability, or embracing innovative designs, the key lies in understanding your audience and staying authentic to your brand's story.

Importance of Sustainable Design

Sustainability in fashion is no longer optional. The fashion industry significantly impacts global ecosystems, contributing approximately 10% of global carbon emissions and 20% of wastewater. Sustainable design mitigates this by employing practices such as utilising recycled or biodegradable materials, adopting circular production models, and reducing water and energy consumption during manufacturing.

The apparel industry, often celebrated for its creativity and dynamism, is increasingly being called upon to balance its innovative spirit with a commitment to sustainability. As environmental and social issues like climate change, resource depletion, and worker exploitation take centre stage, consumers and stakeholders demand that brands rethink their approach to design. Sustainable product design has emerged as a pivotal strategy, blending innovation with responsibility to create desirable and ethical products.

Sustainable product design involves conscious choices at every stage of a product's lifecycle. It requires a holistic view, from selecting eco-friendly materials to ensuring ethical production and planning for end-of-life products. Brands must meet these expectations without stifling creativity or innovation. However, this dual focus is not just a challenge—it's an opportunity.

The benefits of adopting sustainable design practices extend beyond environmental impact. Studies show that consumers increasingly prioritise sustainability in their purchasing decisions. Furthermore, innovations like biodegradable fabrics, circular fashion models, and digital tools for resource optimisation are transforming sustainability into a competitive advantage.

Brands that lead in this space showcase how sustainability can fuel creativity rather than hinder it. For instance, **Patagonia's Worn Wear initiative**, which encourages repair and reuse, exemplifies a circular economy model that resonates with environmentally conscious consumers. Meanwhile, **Adidas' Futurecraft Loop**, a fully recyclable running shoe, demonstrates how cutting-edge innovation can coexist with eco-consciousness.

For entrepreneurs in the fashion industry, embracing sustainable design isn't optional—it's the foundation for long-term success. By embedding sustainability into their product strategies, new brands can differentiate themselves in a crowded market, build customer loyalty, and contribute to a better world.

The journey towards sustainable product design involves transforming ideas, materials, and industry practices. It's about reducing harm and creating meaningful, lasting value. Sustainability and innovation are inseparable companions on the path to redefining the future of fashion.

Best Practices in Sustainable Design

1. **Material Innovation**: Using fabrics like organic cotton, recycled polyester, and alternative materials like mushroom leather (mycelium) reduces reliance on finite resources.

   Mirum: A material made from oceanic matter.

   Circulose: A fabric made from food waste.

   Banana Tex: A material derived from banana leaves.

   Tencel Lyocell: A sustainable material made from wood pulp.

For many years, material innovation in fashion has primarily focused on upcycling textile waste and creating alternatives to genuine leather. (The latter requires a carbon-intensive process, and overconsumption is tied to deforestation.) Now, the conversation has become more granular, more concerned with the actual fibres — specifically, "replacing synthetic fibres in yarns with natural or recyclable ones," says Alan Lugo, director of footwear strategy at Natural Fiber Welding (NFW). This requires a "dramatic diversification of our resources," per

Callaghan: “To maintain and create prosperity for our futures, it means dispersing the reliance on the various organisms and raw materials.”

Companies like Keel Labs and TomTex have stepped in to address that need. Keel Labs’ algae-based seaweed biopolymers, Kelsun, look and feel like natural fibre and have already appeared in collections by Stella McCartney. TomTex uses shrimp shells and mushrooms to create proprietary materials that mimic leather, suede, latex, and more. It has already worked with Peter Do on its faux leather for Spring 2023 and Dauphinette on its handbags for fall 2024.

Cactus and Apple leathers entered the market as buzzy alternatives to cowhide, making it possible to tote around a “leather” bucket bag or coat and feel good about it — but here’s the catch: Lugo says, Leather alternatives like these still rely heavily on polyester and only use the natural product as filler. [They’re] incrementally better, but [are not] fundamentally solving the problem of getting plastics out of those materials.

The emphasis now is on making 100% bio-based materials. “We truly believe that green chemistry and using something that already exists as an input to produce material is the best way to move forward,” Tran explains. “We use chitosan, the most abundant [biopolymer] on earth, and mix it with green substances to create our material. It’s a hundred percent bio-based, so no plastic or petrochemical ingredients exist. It’s naturally biodegradable as well.”

NFW is similarly focused on entirely plant-based materials. Take the company’s Mirum, which is made of natural rubber, plant-based oil, and minerals. It can be used in everything from fashion to furniture to cars, helping reduce the need to rely on plastics and leather at scale. “We try to leverage the abundance of nature’s materials and existing infrastructure as much as possible," Lugo adds.

"If you don't make something accessible and affordable, you won't make any impact — it's going to be just a few small collections, and that's not what the industry needs to move forward," Tran argues. "We want the technology to be a real solution moving forward." A principle for TomTex is that "all the inputs and ingredients need to have a perfect price point so that when you add everything together, the price can be similar to the conventional material that we want to replace."

Rootfull is a company that develops textiles by modifying the growth of wheatgrass roots to create functional fabrics. The origins are cultivated in 3D-printed templates carved from beeswax, where technology meets nature to guide them as they grow. In just 12 days, the seed sprouts, and the root binds to form a naturally woven structure.

Detox Bio Embellishment is a material reminiscent of traditional sequins, but instead of petroleum-based microplastics, it's derived from food waste and fungi. To create this material, fungi are first added to the wastewater from dyeing textiles. Next, the remaining liquid is cured to create this plastic-like material in amber and ruby-red shades.

What if your clothes were another part of your skincare routine? Bio Coterie material innovation, which initially started as a research project exploring the medical applications of biomaterials, hopes to encourage a dialogue around the purpose of materials in the fashion industry.

Imagine clothes that could heal your skin. Combining microalgae and bacterial cellulose, Biocoterie investigates how to grow material that can repair wounds. "There is (an understandable) fear around microbes and how they interact with us," the founder of Bio Coterie, Namita Bhatnagar, tells *GRAZIA*. "But they're everywhere... just because their life cycles don't always visibly manifest around us doesn't mean they're not around pulling massive weight." This material development is in its speculative stage, yet it presents an intriguing outlook on designing with nature.

2. **Circular Design Principles**: Creating garments with end-of-life recyclability or upcycling potential ensures products stay in the value chain longer. Brands like Patagonia excel by encouraging repairs and reselling pre-owned items.

Together, brands, mills, and manufacturers from high street to luxury retailers have proven that circular fashion design can become the norm through the foundation's flagship demonstration project, The Jeans Redesign (2019-2023).

Now, we must not only redesign the products of the future but also transform the systems that deliver them and **keep them in use.** Circular business models designed to keep products in use – such as rental, resale, repair

Remaking allows companies to generate revenue without producing new clothes, representing an opportunity for new and improved growth in the fashion industry.

The fashion industry is rooted in reinvention, and it has the opportunity to reinvent processes, supply chains, and services to decouple revenue from resource use.

Collaboration is key. Working with partners across the supply chain, securing buy-in from leaders, and sharing knowledge creates the conditions for broader, industry-wide change.

Family-owned Cross Textiles has been producing clothes since 1939 and jeans since 1975, supplying major fashion brands worldwide. As a participant in The Jeans Redesign project, the manufacturer has met all the mandatory guidelines on the reported jeans, including avoiding harmful chemicals and techniques in the finishing process and using at least 98% cellulose-based fibres. Peter Lantz, Head of Sustainability at Cross Textiles, describes, "It's firstly a mindset, actions start at the design level. Understanding the 'why' behind the design guidelines empowers designers to become more creative. Everything is less difficult once the customer and we, as a garment manufacturer, align on what we aim to achieve."

Having familiarised themselves with the design principles of a circular economy, the company's garment designers are now expanding the use of The Jeans Redesign guidelines to other garments in its portfolio, such as denim jackets and dresses.

Design is a critical lever in the transition to a circular economy. Meaningful choices are made at the design stage, including product material and how easily they can be reused, repaired, refurbished, or disassembled. This ties into offering circular business models to ensure garments can be returned to a circular system. However, it's hard to reverse the impacts of design decisions once they are implemented – we can't unscramble an omelette.

In the USA, 66% of textiles are sent to landfills, often because clothes are made of complex yarns, for which the processing technology or infrastructure does not exist, let alone in the produced volumes.

By designing clothes to be durable (so that they can be used more), deconstructible (so that the materials they contain can be reused in other garments), and made from safe, recycled, or renewable inputs, Cross Textiles is contributing to the transition to a circular economy for fashion.

3. **Transparency and Traceability**: Incorporating blockchain technology allows brands to track materials and production processes, enhancing consumer trust.

In a world where sustainability is not just a buzzword, but a mandate, transparency and traceability have emerged as game-changers in the fashion industry. These principles empower brands to unveil the hidden layers of their supply chains, fostering trust and accountability in a market increasingly dominated by eco-conscious consumers. Transparency is about being open with consumers regarding sourcing, production practices, and environmental impact. Traceability, on the other hand, involves mapping and documenting the journey of a product from raw material to finished goods.

Today, consumers demand more than style – they want values. Global consumers are willing to adjust their purchasing habits to favour brands committed to sustainability. Moreover, most millennials and Gen Z shoppers prioritise brands that align with their ethical and environmental beliefs. Transparency bridges the gap between a brand's promises and its practices, giving customers the confidence to support businesses that share their values.

From Patagonia's *Footprint Chronicles* to Eileen Fisher's *Renew* programme, leading brands are setting benchmarks by providing detailed insights into their processes. Even fast-fashion giants like H&M are disclosing supplier lists and emphasising sustainable collections to meet the rising demand for ethical production.

For new fashion entrepreneurs, embracing transparency isn't just a moral imperative—it's a competitive advantage. Implementing tools like blockchain for supply chain tracking or collaborating with third-party certifications such as GOTS or Fair Trade can establish credibility. As the fashion industry faces heightened regulatory scrutiny and evolving consumer expectations, transparency and traceability aren't just trends—they're the future of ethical business. They represent a commitment to balancing profits with purpose, ensuring every thread in the fabric of fashion tells a story of accountability and care.

1. Patagonia: A Gold Standard in Traceability

Patagonia is renowned for its transparent supply chain. Its *Footprint Chronicles* initiative allows customers to trace every product's journey, detailing where and how it's made, including labour conditions and environmental impacts. By sharing the ecological cost of its products openly, Patagonia reinforces its commitment to sustainability and ethical sourcing, fostering deep consumer trust.

2. Eileen Fisher: Tackling Waste and Transparency

Eileen Fisher, a leader in sustainable fashion, provides detailed reports on material sourcing and labour practices. The brand's *Renew* programme takes back used clothing for resale or recycling, and its *Vision2020* project outlines goals for 100% organic cotton use and carbon neutrality. Transparency in these initiatives ensures stakeholders remain engaged and informed.

3. H&M Group: Supply Chain Transparency

H&M Group publishes a detailed supplier list, revealing data on the factories producing its garments. Its *Conscious Collection* includes items from sustainably sourced materials like organic cotton and recycled polyester. While H&M faces scrutiny over "greenwashing," its supply chain disclosures mark a step towards greater accountability.

- **Regulatory Push:** The EU's *Sustainable textile Strategy* mandates traceability systems for textile companies to ensure environmental and labour compliance.

Best Practices for Entrepreneurs

1. **Leverage Technology:** Use blockchain to provide immutable records of product journeys from raw materials to retail.
2. **Engage with Stakeholders:** Share supply chain data with consumers through QR codes or digital platforms.
3. **Certifications Matter:** Work with organisations like Fair Trade or the Global Organic Textile Standard (GOTS) for verified sustainability claims.

Visual Aid: Transparency Framework

A visual chart can showcase traceability layers, starting from material sourcing, production, distribution, and post-consumer recycling, illustrating how information flows across the supply chain.

By integrating transparency and traceability, fashion entrepreneurs can build authentic, accountable brands that resonate with conscious consumers and adapt to an increasingly regulated market.

Industry Examples

1. **Stella McCartney**: Known for pioneering sustainable luxury, the brand uses innovative materials like Econyl (regenerated nylon) and promotes circular fashion by collaborating with resale platforms.
2. **H&M's Conscious Collection**: Demonstrates how fast-fashion can integrate sustainable practices, offering affordable, eco-friendly alternatives.
3. **Reformation**: A direct-to-consumer brand that ensures transparency by showcasing the environmental impact of each product on its website.

Market Trends and Consumer Expectations

A 2021 survey by McKinsey found that 67% of consumers consider sustainable materials necessary when purchasing apparel, emphasising the shift towards conscious consumption. Additionally, second-hand fashion markets are booming, projected to reach $77 billion by 2025, as consumers seek sustainable options.

Call to Action for Entrepreneurs

From the article published by McKinsey & Company on Sustainable Style: How Fashion Can Afford and Accelerate Decarbonisation

Fashion brands, big and small, have made ambitious public commitments to creating more sustainable apparel by 2030. However, keeping pace with their commitment to decarbonisation has been a challenge across the industry.

According to a new McKinsey analysis, about two-thirds of brands are behind on their decarbonisation schedules, and 40% have seen their emissions output increase since making their sustainability commitments.

Today, the global fashion industry accounts for an estimated 3 to 8 percent of total greenhouse gas (GHG) emissions, and the industry's emissions are expected to increase by about 30 percent by 2030 if no further action is taken. There's a particular sense of urgency for fashion to decrease emissions as quickly as possible since several countries likely to experience the most significant devastation from climate change are central to fashion's value chain. Intense and frequent weather-related events occur in primary manufacturing countries—such as Bangladesh, China, India, and Vietnam—which export an estimated $65 billion worth of apparel.

Accelerating reduction without affecting the industry is achievable. It could be more affordable than fashion executives think. Our research shows that most fashion brands could reduce their GHG emissions by more than 60 percent for less than 1 to 2 percent of their revenues. (This excludes levers related to reselling, renting, and repairing fashion, which would reduce a brand's emissions intensity significantly but also depend on consumer behaviour shifts.)

Systematic improvements across fashion's value chain can drive progress towards decarbonisation.

New entrants should:

- **Leverage Technology**: Use AI to optimise resource usage and 3D design tools to reduce physical sampling.
- **Adopt Circular Models**: Collaborate with resale or rental platforms to extend product lifespans.
- **Communicate Values**: Product transparency and a straightforward sustainability narrative can differentiate a brand.

Future Outlook

Sustainability is not a passing trend but a necessity. With increasing regulations and consumer awareness, apparel brands that integrate sustainability into their product strategies can drive innovation, foster brand loyalty, and contribute positively to the environment.

Trend and Competitor Analysis

Understanding trends and analysing competitors is helpful and essential for building a resilient product strategy in the dynamic world of fashion. These elements act as your brand's radar, providing insights into shifting consumer behaviours, emerging market opportunities, and potential threats. Even the most creative designs risk missing the mark without a clear grasp of the external landscape.

Fashion trend analysis goes beyond tracking colours or styles; it decodes cultural, economic, and technological influences. A McKinsey report on the *State of Fashion 2023* highlighted the rise of "quiet luxury," where understated yet high-quality products gained traction due to post-pandemic consumer values of longevity and minimalism. Brands like Loro Piana and Bottega Veneta capitalised on this, shaping collections around timeless appeal rather than fleeting fads.

Competitor analysis complements trend insights by helping you identify gaps in the market and refine your unique value proposition. For instance, when Zara introduced its ultra-fast production model, competitors like H&M quickly adapted, balancing speed with sustainability initiatives to stay relevant. Such adaptive strategies emphasise the need for ongoing vigilance in tracking industry leaders and disruptors.

For budding fashion entrepreneurs, mastering these analyses can set the foundation for a differentiated and forward-thinking brand. Tools like Google Trends and platforms such as WGSN offer data-driven insights into global trends, while competitor audits using SWOT frameworks reveal strengths, weaknesses, opportunities, and threats. A Deloitte survey found that 64% of consumers are drawn to brands offering personalised products, emphasising the importance of aligning trend analysis with customer preferences.

Incorporating real-time data, competitor benchmarks, and emerging societal shifts into your strategy ensures your brand is not just following the market but anticipating it. In the fiercely competitive fashion world, trend and competitor analysis are not mere strategies—they're survival tools, turning insights into action and ideas into impact.

There is no one approach to competitor mapping. Every industry is different, and businesses must employ what best suits them.

The types may also vary depending on the kind of campaign, market trends, and competitors you are targeting.

That said, here are the different types of competitor analysis frameworks that are likely to work for your business.

1. Strategic Group Analysis

Your business will face competitors at all levels and use various marketing strategies. To make your team's work more manageable, you must organise your competitors into groups according to their market share, pricing strategies, product offerings, or marketing strategies.

Understand where your business falls in these groups and determine whether adopting their actions can benefit your business. Strategic group analysis works well for companies that are looking to:

- Review their sales and marketing efforts
- Analyse their target market
- Compare their profit margins to those of competitors.

For example, if you're in the hospitality industry, you might want to look at the services your competitors use to lure their customers. For instance, are they offering to pick up and drop off their customers at the airport? What gains is this strategy bringing to their business, and can it also work for you?

2. SWOT Analysis

SWOT stands for Strengths, Weaknesses, Opportunities, and threats. This method evaluates businesses' internal strengths and weaknesses as well as their external opportunities and threats. It can also help you identify your competitors' strengths, weaknesses, opportunities, and threats.

These metrics tell you the following about your competitors:

- Strengths: The strengths refer to what gives your competitors a competitive advantage over yours. They can be reliable customer service, effective marketing, or dedicated staff. Competitor strengths can pose a risk to your business or might point you to some insights for improvement.
- Weaknesses: These competitors' weaknesses can give your business an advantage. This could be employee turnover, a small budget, or negative consumer reviews.
- Opportunities: Your competitors' opportunities to grow, expand, and increase their customers can threaten your business. A good example is new technology that can grow their customer base.
- Threats are external factors that challenge your competitors and affect your business. They can also challenge your competitor's position in the market, giving you an advantage.

SWOT analysis is a good framework for studying your competitors' strengths and opportunities and adopting them in your business. The weaknesses and threats can give you a chance to get ahead.

3. Porter's Five Forces

Michael Porter, the professor behind this framework, believes that there are five forces affecting businesses. They include:

- Competition/rivalry: These are your business's competitors and how their existence affects you.
- Buyer power is the number of buyers your business has and how they affect different things, such as pricing.
- Supplier power: These are your clients. How do they affect your pricing?
- Substitutes: Is there another product that your customers might prefer over yours, even when they have the same qualities? What is the pricing of those substitute products?

- New entrants: As more and more people enter the industry, they may also affect your business. Is it easy for them to lose the market?

Porter's Five Forces works well for businesses starting or planning a new marketing strategy. It helps them better understand the industry's competitive structure. For example, if their product has substitutes, they can find a way to make theirs stand out.

4. Growth-Share Matrix

The Growth-Share Matrix is an assessment tool that helps you determine your business's competitiveness based on different metrics. You can then decide which categories to give high priority to and which ones to ditch. This framework works well for companies with large product portfolios. The metrics used here are:

- Stars: These products or services command a significant market share and growth, so businesses should invest more.
- Question marks: These are products with high growth but low market share. Your business needs to monitor them and decide whether to invest more or abandon them.
- Cash cows: These products have limited growth potential but command a high market share.
- Pets: These have a low growth and market share but are essential. Your business can decide to rebrand or abandon them.

This framework for competitor market analysis helps businesses decide which competitors are worth their attention and investment. They'll understand which ones are helping them grow, expand their market shares, and make informed decisions.

5. Perceptual Mapping

The perceptual mapping framework, or positioning mapping, helps your business understand how customers perceive competitors.

It compares your brand to your competitor in a graph using two factors. Often, companies choose to determine the positioning or perception of a product's quality and price.

What's the price of your product compared to its quantity? What is your competitor's cost and the amount of the same product or service? With your answer, you can identify gaps in market trends and make adjustments where necessary.

For example, if you're offering a high-quality product at a lower price than your competitors, you can consider increasing the cost.

6. PEST Analysis

A PESTLE analysis is a tool that gives valuable insights into an industry's overall macro environment. PESTLE stands for six political, economic, social, technological, legal, and environmental factors. These factors are helpful as they help to determine the external influences that can impact businesses.

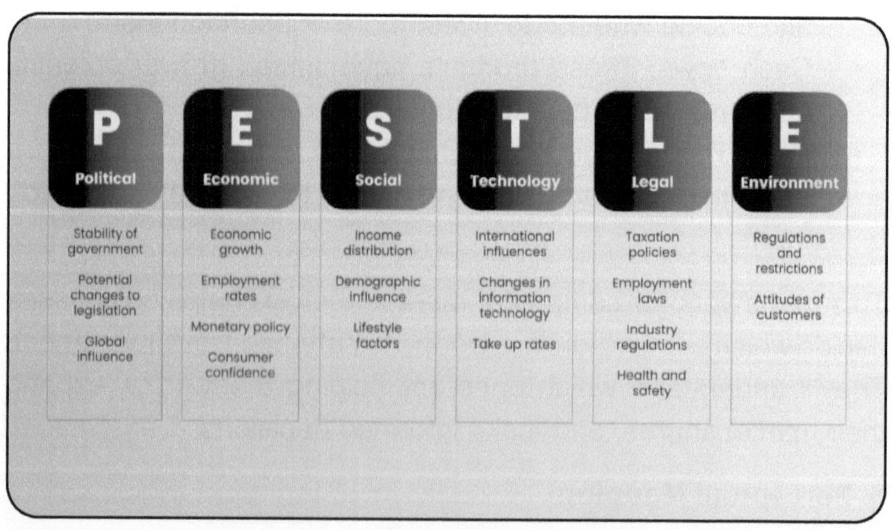

Source: Windmill Digital

Below, we examine these factors further:

Political: These are linked to the government's control and influence over a country's economy and market. Some examples of government factors are legislative or economic policies. Having a good knowledge of the political environment of a country is important because it can affect the industry in many ways. These include but are not limited to trade tariffs, increased taxation, fiscal policies, etc.

Economic factors directly affect a company's long-term prospects. A company's financial environment can impact its product prices and supply and demand. Some examples of economic factors include rising inflation rates, unemployment, and high foreign exchange rates.

Social factors include cultural norms, health awareness, population growth rate, and career attitudes. These factors are pivotal in helping companies develop their marketing strategies, especially targeting specific customers.

Technological: These factors are linked to technological developments that affect a company's operations. Take advanced technological advancements like artificial intelligence or deep learning, for example. If companies in this day and age fail to live up to these trends or aren't fully aware of them, they might weaken their position in the market. PESTLE analysis deals with technological factors like infrastructure development, the pace of technological advancements, etc.

Legal factors include changes in legislative policies that affect employment, access to adequate resources, tax levels, and other aspects of the business environment. These factors are essential to consider.

Environmental factors are linked to the ecological aspects of an environment. They include, but are not limited to, water disposal rules and regulations, energy consumption laws, and more. The environmental aspect of PESTLE is especially applicable to industries like tourism and agriculture.

The following steps will help simplify the process of conducting a PESTLE analysis:

Brainstorm: Reflect on the various facets of the business that are directly linked to PESTLE. Consider the positive or negative impacts and how to incorporate this data into the analysis. For a greater perspective, consider seeking advice from experts outside the industry.

Research: Conduct extensive research for each PESTLE analysis part and look for supporting evidence for each insight. D&B Hoovers, for example, is a data company that provides information necessary to analyse a business's risks.

Evaluate: Rate the likelihood of every factor in the PESTLE analysis and how it can impact the business.

Refine: Repeat this process until you have reduced it to a practical number of articulated and clear points in all the categories of PESTLE.

7. Customer Journey

A customer journey map shows how customers interact with your brand from when they first discover it to when they take the desired action. This framework also examines the channels a customer uses to reach your brand, including social media, email marketing, and face-to-face interactions.

The customer journey framework can provide other metrics, such as the number of followers, phone calls, or email replies. It can also be used to check how your competitors interact with their customers and how responsive they are to inquiries. Using this insight, you can identify opportunities to improve your brand.

8. 7P's Marketing Model

7Ps, also known as the marketing mix, show the products that a business is selling and how they're doing it. You can use this model for your brand or to analyse your competitors.

The 7Ps stand for:

- Product
- Price
- Place
- Promotion
- People
- Process
- Physical evidence

If you're a business selling products, you can use the 7Ps to analyse, create, and revamp your marketing strategies. By understanding your competitors' 7Ps, you can develop your value proposition.

Advantages of Using a Competitor Analysis Framework

- Find trends, patterns, and shifts: Understanding what's happening in the industry is crucial to developing your business.
- Discover gaps you weren't aware of: The frameworks will help you understand the marketing gaps your team is missing. You can discover a new idea, product, or sales strategy.

- Create an effective marketing roadmap strategy: Knowing what works and what doesn't work for your competitors helps you develop a more effective marketing roadmap strategy for your business.
- Build specific and measurable goals: From the competitor data, your business can develop specific and measurable goals that will bring results.
- Avoid mistakes: The frameworks also help you learn from your competitors' mistakes along the way. You can learn from their mistakes and avoid making the same in your business.
- Quickly review data: These frameworks work with visual tools such as maps, graphs, charts, etc., which make it easy to review and analyse data. You can easily discuss them with your marketing team or investors if they're presented in a visually appealing manner.

What are fashion trends?

A fashion trend is a style that becomes popular during a particular period and is often influenced by cultural background, historical events, social influences, or technological advancements. Designers and influencers usually spread trends, and they play a massive role in the fashion industry by driving consumer demand and creating new opportunities for creativity.

Fashion trend forecasting considers anticipating upcoming fashion trends by analysing multiple factors, such as:

- Consumer habits,
- Social and cultural movements,
- Historical data,
- Runway collections,
- Social media content,
- Urban fashion and pop culture,

- Textile and material innovations,
- Global economic and political events,
- Sustainability and ethical considerations, etc.

Trend forecasters leverage this information to deliver insights and direction to designers and labels about the styles expected to be most popular in the future.

How can new trends be forecasted?

Fashion forecasting is essential to establish guidelines for the fashion business. To understand how trends will emerge, there are various fashion trend forecasting methods that trend forecasters rely on, and they include:

- Studying past and current fashion trends via market research, consumer surveys, and sales data analysis.
- Trusting fashion industry experts such as designers, stylists, and fashion forecasters with enough knowledge to anticipate future trends.
- Looking at runway shows and street style for inspiration about new trends that fashion brands will adopt in trend forecasting.
- Analysing cultural and social influences such as music, art, politics, technology, and worldwide events.

By analysing this information, trend forecasters can accurately predict which styles will be the trendiest in the future.

Researching sTrends in Magazines

The first method possible in trend forecasting is researching magazines because they dictate macro trends. That means fashion magazines like Vogue, Harper's Bazaar, and Elle publish exclusive previews, insider information, and content from fashion shows, street styles, or cultural movements, becoming great for tracking future trends.

To effectively research a fashion trend in a magazine, the following steps should be considered:

1. Searching for publications that focus on fashion, beauty, and lifestyle.
2. Reviewing the content from the perspective of a fashion forecaster by considering factors such as the target audience, industry validation, season, and longevity and separating long-term and short-term forecasting.
3. Evaluating trends and analysing key elements like colours, fabrics, shapes, textures, and visual designs.
4. Keeping track of the trend by making notes, creating a mood board, or using a digital platform to save images and articles.
5. Seeking out trend variations based on region, season, and age group.

Analyse the season's colour palette by studying the standard colours presented by all fashion brands. For example, every season has a specific Pantone colour.

Look for recurring themes in shapes, silhouettes, fabrics, accessories, and trims.

Pay attention to details like unique embellishments, prints, or textures.

Consider the overall mood of the collections (e.g., whether they are romantic, punk, nostalgic, etc.). This may help with trend forecasting for the upcoming fashion year.

Trend forecasting agencies in the fashion industry

Trend forecasting agencies are essential because they produce trend research reports based on consumer habits and current events. They provide valuable insights into upcoming fashion trends and disseminate them to the global supply chains in the fashion industry.

WGSN

WGSN is the world's leading authority in forecasting trends for the fashion, beauty, and lifestyle industries. It accurately forecasts trends using data and global, cross-industry expert knowledge, covering everything from social media and catwalk shows to e-commerce, search, and consumer sentiment. With its trend reports and mood boards, WGSN helps clients, from small startups to large multinational corporations, stay informed and competitive in their respective markets.

Heuritech

Heuritech uses artificial intelligence to provide trend forecasts to businesses. The technology analyses millions of real-world images shared on social media, e-commerce websites, and fashion blogs into meaningful insights.

The artificial intelligence Heuritech uses in trend research helps brands stay competitive and meet consumer demands.

Trendzoom

Trendzoom's long-term forecasting provides robust information to apparel and accessories companies. Its experts include fashion forecasters, designers, and industry insiders. Trendzoom offers other services such as trade show reports and bespoke trend analysis.

Patternbank

Unlike most trend forecasters, Patternbank specialises in prints and pattern trends for the fashion, textiles, and interior design industries. It is the go-to virtual textile studio platform because it offers a streamlined service where customers can discover curated designs, obtain trend forecasting inspiration, and directly download digital files.

THE DONEGER GROUP

The Doneger Group is a long-term forecasting and creative strategy consultancy that delivers business and innovative strategies for branding and positioning, consumer engagement, merchandising and curation, design direction, and marketing and messaging.

FASHION SNOOPS

Fashion Snoops helps fashion, accessories, home decor, beauty, and other brands forecast trends. The company offers a subscription-based online platform with trend reports, inspiration, and tailored consulting services to support clients' specific needs in the fashion market.

Trend Council

Trend Council provides long-term and short-term forecasting, runway analysis, colour and pattern analysis, retail reporting, and design inspiration to partner consultants, premium retailers, designers, buyers, and merchandisers worldwide.

BoF

Business of Fashion is a media and analysis company that provides news, analysis, and insights to fashion industry professionals. It aims to inform, inspire, and connect the global fashion community through articles, videos, podcasts, and newsletters.

BoF's mission is translated into fashion forecasting, as it is always looking for new concepts and future ideas.

Key Takeaways from the Chapter:

1. **The Power of Product Positioning**
    - Product positioning is essential for creating a unique identity and emotional connection with customers.
    - Successful brands focus on values and lifestyles that resonate deeply with their target audience—differentiation as a Survival Tool.
    - In the fast-changing apparel industry, standing out is critical to success.
    - Differentiation involves answering the questions: *What makes your brand unique?* and *What emotional need does it address?*
    - Strategies include innovative materials, exceptional customer experiences, and compelling brand narratives.
2. **Best Practices for Differentiation in Apparel**
    - **Value-Based Differentiation:** Align offerings with customer values (e.g. Patagonia's eco-conscious practices).
    - **Niche Focus:** Tailor products to specific market segments to create strong loyalty (e.g., Decathlon's sports-specific focus).
    - **Quality and Craftsmanship:** Emphasise superior materials and production (e.g. Levi's durable denim).
    - **Innovative Design:** Introduce cutting-edge functionality and aesthetics (e.g. Uniqlo's HeatTech fabric).
3. **Customer-Centric Approach**
    - Understand and prioritise customer needs through research and feedback.
    - Use personalisation to enhance relevance and build trust.
    - Ensure consistency across all customer touchpoints for a unified experience.

4. **Importance of Sustainable Product Design**
   - Sustainable design mitigates the apparel industry's environmental and social impact.
   - Practices like using biodegradable materials, circular production, and reduced resource consumption are becoming essential.
   - Brands like Patagonia and Adidas demonstrate how sustainability and innovation coexist, offering a competitive advantage.

5. **Key Lessons for Entrepreneurs**
   - Focus on your brand's purpose to connect emotionally with your audience.
   - Invest in innovation to differentiate your products.
   - Embrace sustainable design as both a responsibility and an opportunity to build long-term success.

New fashion brands can compete and thrive in today's marketplace by combining product positioning, differentiation, customer-centricity, and sustainability.

Material Innovation

- **Emerging Materials**: Organic cotton, recycled polyester, and alternatives like mushroom leather (mycelium), Mirum (ocean matter), Circulose (food waste), BananaTex (banana leaves), and Tencel Lyocell (wood pulp) reduce reliance on finite resources.
- **Focus on Fibre**: The shift from leather alternatives to replacing synthetic fibres with natural or recyclable options emphasises diversifying material resources.
- **Bio-Based Innovations**: Companies like TomTex (shrimp shells, mushrooms) and NFW (natural rubber, plant-

based oil) are pioneering 100% biodegradable, plastic-free materials.

- **Economic Accessibility**: Sustainable innovations must align with competitive prices to scale and replace conventional materials effectively.

Circular Design Principles

- **Design for Longevity**: Durable, deconstructible, and safe materials ensure products remain within the value chain longer.
- **Systems Transformation**: Circular business models (rental, resale, repair) decouple revenue growth from resource consumption, enabling sustainable expansion.
- **Design Mindset**: Waste minimisation and durability should be integral to the product development stage.

Transparency and Traceability

- **Consumer Trust**: Openly sharing supply chain information through tools like blockchain builds credibility and aligns with eco-conscious consumer expectations.
- **Practical Steps for Entrepreneurs**:

  Implement blockchain for supply chain tracking.

  - Obtain certifications like Fair Trade or GOTS to validate sustainability claims.
  - Engage consumers with QR codes or digital platforms to share supply chain data.

Future Outlook

- **Decarbonisation Challenges**: Despite ambitious commitments, two-thirds of fashion brands are behind schedule. Without action, industry emissions could rise by 30% by 2030.

- **Strategic Interventions**
    - **AI and 3D Design**: Reduces waste in physical sampling and optimises resource use.
    - **Circular Models**: Collaborate with resale and rental platforms to extend product lifespans.
    - **Clear Messaging**: Transparency and sustainability storytelling enhance brand differentiation.

By adopting sustainable practices, leveraging innovative materials, and prioritising transparency, fashion entrepreneurs can build resilient brands that meet consumer demand and regulatory requirements while reducing environmental impact.

Trend and Competitor Analysis

1. Importance of Trend and Competitor Analysis

- These tools provide insights into consumer behaviour, market opportunities, and threats.
- They are essential for building resilient product strategies and creating differentiated brands.

2. Fashion Trend Analysis

- It goes beyond surface-level trends like colours or styles and considers cultural, economic, and technological influences.
- Trend analysis helps brands anticipate rather than react to market demands.

3. Competitor Analysis

- Identifies market gaps and refines value propositions.
- Tools like Google Trends, SWOT analysis, and platforms such as WGSN offer actionable insights.

4. Frameworks for Competitor Analysis

- **Strategic Group Analysis**: Groups competitors by factors like market share or pricing strategies to evaluate sales efforts and identify opportunities.
- **SWOT Analysis**: Examines strengths, weaknesses, opportunities, and threats for both your brand and competitors.
- **Porter's Five Forces** analyzes competition, buyer/supplier power, substitutes, and barriers to new entrants.
- **Growth-Share Matrix**: Categorises products as stars, cash cows, question marks, or pets to prioritise investments.
- **Perceptual Mapping**: Helps visualise customer perception of a brand relative to competitors.
- **PEST Analysis**: Review macro factors (political, economic, social, technological, legal, environmental) influencing the business environment.
- **Customer Journey Mapping**: Examines how customers interact with a brand and identifies areas for improvement.
- **7P's Marketing Model**: Analyses product, Price, Place, Promotion, People, Process, and Physical evidence.

5. Advantages of Using Frameworks

- Uncover trends, patterns and gaps in the market.
- Enable the creation of effective marketing strategies and measurable goals.
- Provide visual tools for quick data review and strategic discussions.
- Avoid competitors' mistakes and refine business strategies.

6. Fashion Trend Forecasting

- It involves predicting styles based on consumer habits, cultural movements, historical data, and technological innovations.
- Methods include analysing magazines, runway shows, and social media using expert insights and technological tools.

7. Notable Trend Forecasting Agencies

- **WGSN**: Industry leader offering data-driven insights.
- **Heuritech:** AI-based trend forecasting through social media and digital content analysis.
- **Trendzoom, Patternbank, Doneger Group, Fashion Snoops, Trend Council, BoF**: Agencies providing specialised forecasting services tailored to various fashion sectors.

Chapter 6

Crafting an Unforgettable Brand Identity

"Building a Brand People Feel, Not Just See"

In the ever-evolving, fiercely competitive fashion world, establishing a brand identity that resonates and endures is more crucial than ever. The chapter delves deep into the art and science of creating a distinctive brand identity that captures the essence of your fashion brand and forges a lasting emotional connection with your audience.

The journey to build an unforgettable brand identity begins with understanding the core elements that define your brand. From visual components such as logos, colour schemes, and typography to intangible elements like brand voice and values, each aspect plays a pivotal role in shaping how your audience perceives you. According to a survey conducted by Brandwatch, 91% of consumers are more likely to buy from an authentic brand than a generic one[22]. This statistic underscores the importance of authenticity in crafting your brand identity. I want to mention the story of the creation of Nike's logo here.

The Nike swoosh logo was created in 1971 by Carolyn Davidson, a graphic design student at Portland State University. She was

22 The Power of Brand Authenticity on social media [Infographic] **Authenticity can inspire trust and loyalty -- and drive ROI.**

approached by Phil Knight, co-founder of Nike (then known as Blue Ribbon Sports), who was teaching at the university and needed a logo for his new athletic shoe brand. Davidson designed the swoosh, which symbolises motion and speed and reflects the wings of Nike, the Greek goddess of victory. Knight paid her $35 for the design, which equated to about 17.5 hours of work at $2 per hour.

Knight wasn't overly enthusiastic about the design but decided to proceed. Over time, the swoosh became a cornerstone of Nike's brand identity and a globally recognised symbol of athletic excellence. In 1983, as Nike's success skyrocketed, the company honoured Davidson by gifting her a diamond ring, chocolate replicas of the swoosh, and company stock, which later grew to be worth over $1 million.

The swoosh's success lies in its simplicity, versatility, and ability to convey energy and movement. Coupled with strategic marketing and endorsements by high-profile athletes, it became a cultural and global icon.[23] Nike's swoosh is more than a design—it represents movement, excellence, and athleticism. These brands have mastered the art of aligning their visual identity with their core values, creating a powerful, recognisable presence in the market.

Consider Chanel, the iconic example. The interlocking "CC" logo is not just a symbol; it's a statement of luxury, elegance, and timeless fashion.

---

23 The Fascinating Journey of the Nike Logo - 12&28 Creative Studio

To illustrate, let's examine a case study of an emerging fashion brand: Everlane. Everlane has built a loyal customer base that values ethical practices and quality by emphasising radical transparency about its pricing and production processes. This alignment of brand values with consumer expectations has been pivotal in its growth, as shown by its 200% increase in revenue since 2017.

When I was working for Louis Philippe, a Luxury Apparel Brand in India, I was part of the launch of the Sports Brand under Louis Philippe. As the Brand was already commanding India's most premium Brand status, they wanted to ensure the Brand Guidelines were clearly defined. To do this, the management appointed a consultant from the US who was well-known for creating branding and setting the standards for a brand. The in-depth analysis and time spent finalising the logo, Brand colours, packaging, Marketing content, and visual identity is commendable. There was no hurry in just launching a Brand; they were not interested in creating just another Brand, but they wanted to launch a well-crafted Brand that lives with the ethos of the parent Brand but lives younger and caters to a lower age group of customers.

This chapter will explore actionable strategies to define and articulate your brand's unique identity. Through real-world examples, detailed insights, and practical exercises, you'll learn how to create a brand that not only stands out but also stands the test of time.

1. Visual Identity Components

How do you create a distinctive logo?

A logo is often the first point of visual contact between your brand and potential customers. It embodies your brand's essence, values, and aesthetics in a single image. Here's how to create a logo that stands out and effectively communicates your brand's identity.

1. Understand Your Brand

Before diving into design, it's crucial to have a deep understanding of your brand. What are your core values, mission, and vision? What emotions do you want your brand to evoke? For example, a luxury brand might focus on elegance and sophistication, while a streetwear brand might emphasise boldness and urban culture.

2. Research and Inspiration

Look at the logos of successful fashion brands to understand what works. Analyse how brands like Chanel, Nike, and Louis Vuitton use simplicity, symbols, and typography. Chanel's interlocking "CC" logo is a classic example of a simple yet powerful design. According to a study by FinancesOnline, the best brand names are made up of words or acronyms, showing that simplicity often leads to recognition.

3. Design Principles

- **Simplicity**: A simple logo is easily recognisable and versatile. Think of the minimalist approach used by brands like Gucci and Burberry.
- **Memorability**: Your logo should be distinctive enough to be remembered. Unique elements and clever design play a significant role here.
- **Relevance**: The logo should be relevant to your brand's industry and target audience. For example, athletic brands often incorporate elements of movement or speed in their logos.
- **Versatility**: It should look good in various sizes and formats, whether on a billboard or a business card.

4. Use of Colours

Colours evoke emotions and convey messages. The fashion industry uses colour extensively, black often signifies luxury, red represents boldness, and green denotes sustainability. A survey by Colour Matters shows that colours can increase brand recognition by up to 80%.

5. Typography

Choose fonts that reflect your brand's personality. Serif fonts convey tradition and reliability, while sans-serif fonts are modern and clean. For instance, the sans-serif font used by Calvin Klein reflects its modern and minimalistic approach.

6. Feedback and Iteration

Once you have a few design drafts, seek feedback from your target audience. This can provide valuable insights into how your logo is perceived. According to a study by the Design Council, companies that emphasise design perform 200% better than those that do not.

7. Professional Assistance

Consider hiring a professional graphic designer. While DIY tools are available, a professional can bring expertise and creativity to the table, ensuring your logo is attractive and strategically sound.

- **Apple:** Rob Janoff's Apple logo is an excellent example of simplicity and memorability. Despite its simplicity, it conveys a sense of innovation and quality.
- **Nike:** Carolyn Davidson designed the Nike "swoosh," another iconic logo. The swoosh represents movement and speed, perfectly aligning with the brand's focus on athletic performance.

Element	Description	Example
Logo	A simple, memorable design representing your brand's values and identity.	Chanel's "CC"
Color Palette	Colors that evoke specific emotions and align with your brand's message.	Red for boldness
Typography	Fonts that reflect your brand's personality and style.	Sans-serif for modernity
Symbols	Unique symbols that reinforce your brand's identity.	Nike's "Swoosh"

Creating a distinctive logo involves combining creativity, strategic thinking, and a deep understanding of your brand. By following these guidelines and learning from successful examples, you can develop a logo that stands out and effectively communicates the essence of your fashion brand.

I recently saw a post on X from @hosun_chung. He is the Operating Partner at @thoughtleadrX, and he builds brands on X and beyond for founders. He recently posted research on how the logos of big brands are changing.

His post says below

Notice how logos recently all look the same?

They don't look better, but this psychological trick manipulates your brain. That's why Google, Microsoft and Airbnb do the same thing.

*

Look closely at these new logos. They're not just more straightforward but starting to look eerily similar. Sans-serif fonts, basic shapes, limited colours. It's like they're all following the same hidden playbook. But why? The answer lies in human psychology:

*

Our brains process visuals 60,000 times faster than text. And here's the fascinating part:

The simpler the visual, the faster we process it. This is why companies are racing to simplify their logos. But there's more to this story...

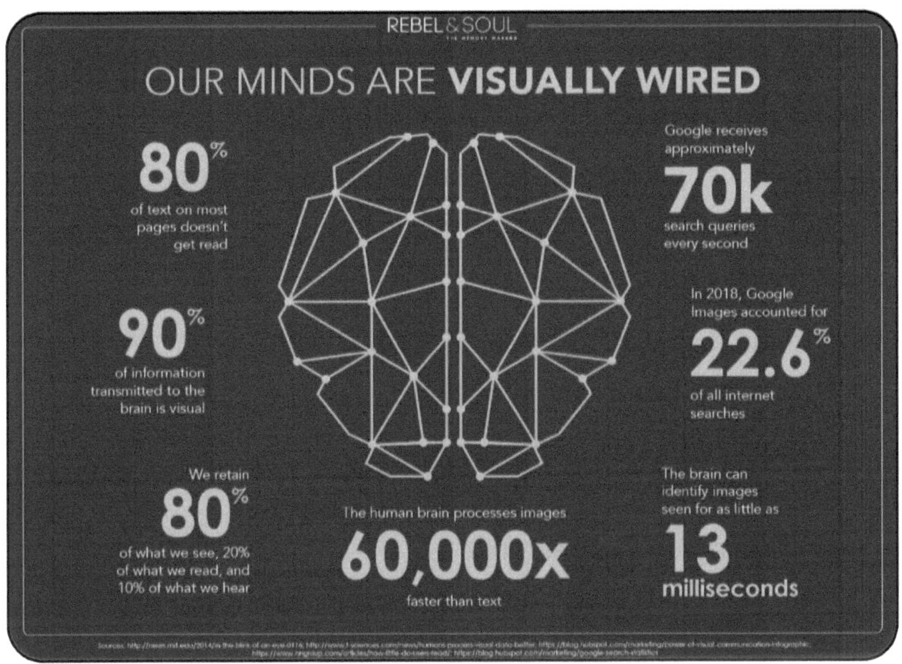

Take Google's evolution:

1999: Complex, shadowed text

2010: Glossy, 3D effects

2015: Flat, sans-serif font

Each iteration became progressively simpler.

42% of consumers perceive brands with modernised logos as more trustworthy.

Microsoft followed a similar path:

- Removed all gradients
  - Eliminated shadows and depth
  - Switched to basic geometric shapes

But the real genius? These weren't just aesthetic choices...

The digital revolution drove these changes.

Logos today need to work across dozens of platforms:

Think of tiny app icons. Social media profiles. Website headers.

And that's just online. The rise of wearables (e.g. Apple Watch) accelerated this trend...

Airbnb's old logo was failing in the digital age:

- Hard to animate
- Illegible at small sizes
- Inconsistent across platforms

It was challenging to remember.

The new logo, despite the initial backlash, solved all these problems.

Here's where it gets interesting:

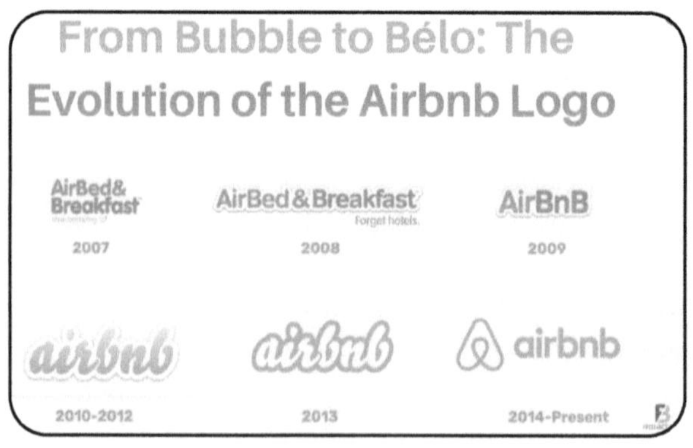

The human brain has a preference for simple shapes.

We're hardwired to remember:

- Straight lines over curves
- Circles around complex polygons
- Basic patterns rather than intricate designs

Simple shapes and colours influence 75% of consumer perceptions.

As logos became simpler to meet these requirements, they started looking more alike.

It's not laziness or lack of creativity.

It's evolution.

This trend isn't slowing down.

More companies are simplifying their logos every year.

Because in a world of infinite content and shrinking attention spans, simplicity isn't just beautiful.

It's survival.

2. Brand Voice and Values

Creating a distinct and consistent brand voice is essential in developing a compelling brand identity. Your brand voice is the personality and tone in which you communicate with your audience, while your brand values are the guiding principles that shape your brand's mission, vision, and interactions. Together, they forge a powerful connection with your audience.

1. Defining Brand Voice

Your brand voice should reflect your brand's personality. Is your brand playful and fun, or is it serious and professional? Consider the difference in tone between brands like Zara, which maintains a sophisticated and polished tone, and Urban Outfitters, which adopts a more casual and quirky style. A survey by Sprout Social found that 40% of consumers say memorable content is the key to making a brand stand out, highlighting the importance of a consistent and unique voice.

2. Consistency Across Channels

Maintaining a consistent brand voice across all platforms—from your website and social media to customer service interactions—is crucial. Consistency builds trust and recognition. For instance, Nike's empowering and motivational tone is consistently present across its advertising, social media, and customer communications.

3. Core Brand Values

Brand values are the ethical and moral principles that guide your brand's actions and decisions. Defining these values helps you align your brand with the expectations and values of your audience. According to a report by Accenture, 63% of consumers prefer to purchase products and services from companies that stand for a purpose that reflects their values and beliefs.

4. Crafting Your Brand Story

Use your brand voice and values to tell a compelling brand story. Your story should reflect your brand's journey, mission, and vision. For example, Patagonia's brand story emphasises environmental activism and sustainability, which resonates deeply with its audience and reinforces its brand values.

- **Dove**: Dove's brand voice is warm, inclusive, and empowering, reflecting its commitment to absolute beauty and self-esteem. The brand's campaigns consistently promote body positivity and diversity, reinforcing its core values.
- **TOMS**: TOMS' brand values centre on social responsibility and giving back. The company's "One for One" campaign, which donates a pair of shoes for every pair sold, aligns perfectly with its mission to improve lives.

Using Data to Refine Your Voice

Conducting surveys and gathering feedback from your audience can provide valuable insights into how your brand voice is perceived. Tools like Net Promoter Score (NPS) can help gauge customer satisfaction and loyalty. A study by Salesforce found that 80% of customers say the experience a company provides is as important as its products and services, underscoring the significance of a well-defined brand voice.[24]

7. Visual Representation

Your brand voice and values should also be reflected visually. Consistent use of colours, fonts, and imagery that align with your brand's tone can enhance recognition and reinforce your

---

24 **Salesforce's State of the Connected Customer report**. You can find more details about this study on the Salesforce website or in their report titled **"Customer Engagement Research 2022"**.

messaging. For example, The North Face's rustic and earthy tones complement its adventurous and outdoorsy brand voice.

Element	Description	Example
Brand Voice	The personality and tone in which your brand communicates.	Urban Outfitters - Casual and Quirky
Core Values	The guiding principles that shape your brand's mission and interactions.	TOMS - Social Responsibility
Consumer Preferences	63% of consumers prefer to buy from brands that reflect their own values and beliefs.	Accenture Report

Crafting a distinct brand voice and clearly defining your brand values is crucial to building a memorable and authentic brand identity. By maintaining consistency across all touchpoints and aligning your messaging with your core principles, you can create a brand that stands out and resonates deeply with your audience.

3. Emotional Connections

- Techniques to create lasting emotional bonds with consumers.
- Utilising consumer psychology in branding strategies.

Emotional Connections: Techniques to Create Lasting Emotional Bonds with Consumers

Building strong emotional connections with consumers is pivotal in creating an unforgettable brand identity. Emotional connections drive loyalty, enhance customer retention, and differentiate your brand in a crowded market. Here's how to effectively develop and leverage these connections.

1. Understanding Emotional Branding

Emotional branding involves creating a deep connection with consumers and fostering brand loyalty and advocacy. It's about evoking specific feelings that resonate with your audience. According to a study by Capgemini, emotionally engaged customers are likely to spend twice as much on brands they are loyal to[25].

2. Techniques to Create Lasting Emotional Bonds

- **Storytelling**: Crafting compelling stories highlighting your brand's values, mission, and vision can create a powerful emotional impact. For instance, TOMS effectively uses storytelling by sharing narratives about their charitable initiatives, fostering a sense of community and purpose among their customers.
- **Personalisation**: Personalised experiences make consumers feel valued and understood. Brands can achieve this through targeted marketing, customised products, and personalised customer service. According to Epsilon, 80% of consumers are more likely to purchase when brands offer personalised experiences.[26]
- **Customer Engagement**: Engaging with your audience through social media, events, and interactive campaigns helps build community and belonging. Nike's engagement through their "Just Do It" campaigns, challenges, and social media interactions fosters a strong emotional bond with their customers.
- **Visual Appeal**: Using colours, imagery, and design can evoke specific emotions. For instance, vibrant and energetic colours can create excitement, while soft and pastel shades

---

25 "Loyalty Deciphered—How Emotions Drive Genuine Engagement"

26 **"The Power of Me: The Impact of Personalisation on Marketing Performance"**

may evoke calmness and tranquillity. A study by Loyola University Maryland suggests that colour increases brand recognition by up to 80%.[27]

3. Utilising Consumer Psychology in Branding Strategies

- **Behavioural Insights**: Understanding consumer behaviour and psychological triggers can help tailor your branding strategies. For example, scarcity and urgency (e.g., limited time offers) can drive consumers to purchase quickly.
- **Emotional Triggers**: Identifying and leveraging emotional triggers such as nostalgia, happiness, and fear can make your branding more impactful. Coca-Cola's "Share a Coke" campaign used personalisation and nostalgia, significantly boosting sales and consumer engagement.
- **Social Proof**: Demonstrating that others trust and love your brand can build credibility and attract new customers. Showcasing testimonials, user-generated content, and influencer endorsements effectively utilises social proof.

Apple: Apple's branding focuses on innovation, simplicity, and a premium lifestyle, creating a strong emotional connection with its customers. The anticipation and excitement around Apple's product launches exemplify the emotional bond between the brand and its audience.

Patagonia emphasises its commitment to environmental sustainability and ethical practices. Its brand values resonate deeply with its audience, fostering loyalty and advocacy. Patagonia's "Don't Buy This Jacket" campaign urged customers to consider the environmental impact of consumerism, reinforcing its values and engaging emotionally with its audience.

---

27 **"Colour increases brand recognition by 80%": the real contents of the Loyola study revealed** 27/02/2019

Emotional Trigger	Impact on Consumer Loyalty	Example Brand
Nostalgia	Increases attachment and engagement	Coca-Cola
Happiness	Promotes positive association and repeat purchases	Disney
Fear (e.g., Missing Out)	Drives urgency and immediate action	Amazon Prime
Community & Belonging	Builds a loyal customer base	Nike

Creating lasting emotional bonds with consumers involves a strategic blend of storytelling, personalisation, and understanding consumer psychology. By leveraging these techniques, your brand can foster deep emotional connections that drive loyalty and differentiate you in the competitive fashion industry.

4. Consistency and Evolution: Maintaining and Adapting Brand Identity

Maintaining a consistent brand identity across various platforms while evolving with market trends and consumer feedback is crucial for sustaining a strong, recognisable brand presence in the fast-paced fashion industry.

1. Maintaining Brand Identity Consistency

Consistency in brand identity ensures that your brand is easily recognisable, regardless of where or how consumers interact. This involves maintaining uniformity in visual elements, messaging, and the overall brand experience across all channels.

- **Visual Consistency**: Ensure that your logo, colour palette, typography, and imagery are consistent across all platforms—your website, social media profiles, packaging, or physical stores. For instance, Louis Vuitton's consistent use of its iconic monogram pattern across products and marketing materials reinforces brand recognition and luxury status.

- **Messaging Consistency**: Your brand voice and messaging should be uniform across all communication channels. This means that the tone and message should feel coherent and aligned if a customer interacts with your brand through an email newsletter, a social media post, or a customer service representative. Nike's empowering and motivational tone remains consistent across its advertisements, social media, and customer interactions.
- **Brand Guidelines**: Develop comprehensive guidelines detailing how your brand should be represented visually and verbally. This document should be a reference for anyone creating content for your brand and ensure consistency in all brand-related materials. A study by Lucidpress found that brands with consistent presentation are three to four times more likely to enjoy excellent brand visibility.

2. Adapting Brand Identity to Market Trends and Consumer Feedback

While consistency is key, flexibility in adapting to new trends and consumer preferences is equally essential. Adapting your brand identity ensures it remains relevant and resonates with your evolving audience.

- **Market Trends**: Stay attuned to industry trends and technological advancements. Adapting to these changes can involve refreshing your visual identity, updating your brand messaging, or introducing new product lines. For example, Burberry's rebranding in 2018, which included a new logo and monogram, aligned with contemporary design trends while maintaining its heritage.
- **Consumer Feedback**: Listen to and incorporate consumer feedback into your brand strategy. This can be done through

surveys, social media interactions, and customer reviews. According to a report by Qualtrics, 89% of companies that lead with customer experience perform better financially than their peers.

- **Evolutionary Rebranding**: Significant shifts in market conditions or consumer expectations sometimes necessitate a brand evolution. This doesn't mean abandoning your core identity but refreshing it to stay relevant. A successful example is Pepsi's various logo evolutions, each reflecting contemporary design trends while retaining brand recognition.

Airbnb: In 2014, Airbnb rebranded with a new logo, updated website, and a refreshed brand voice focused on belonging and community. This modernised the company's visual identity and aligned it with its evolving mission and values.

Starbucks: Starbucks regularly updates its brand elements, such as store designs and packaging, to stay current with market trends while maintaining core brand elements like its green mermaid logo. This balance between consistency and evolution has helped Starbucks remain relevant and popular.

Factor	Impact on Brand Success	Example Brand
Visual Consistency	Enhances brand recognition and trust	Louis Vuitton
Messaging Consistency	Builds a coherent and trustworthy brand presence	Nike
Adaptation to Market Trends	Ensures relevance and resonance with target audience	Burberry
Incorporating Consumer Feedback	Improves customer satisfaction and loyalty	Airbnb

Maintaining a consistent brand identity across various platforms ensures recognition and trust, while adapting to market trends and consumer feedback keeps your brand relevant and connected with your audience. Striking the right balance between consistency and evolution is key to sustaining a strong, impactful brand identity in the dynamic fashion industry.

Examples of Successful Brand Identities in the Fashion Industry

1. **Chanel**

    - **Visual Identity**: Chanel's visual identity is defined by its iconic interlocking "CC" logo, a monochromatic colour palette, and elegant typography. These elements collectively convey luxury, sophistication, and timelessness.
    - **Brand Voice and Values**: Chanel's voice is refined and aspirational, reflecting its commitment to high fashion and exclusivity. The brand values include innovation, classic elegance, and femininity.
    - **Emotional Connection**: Chanel's heritage creates an emotional connection, evoking a sense of glamour and exclusivity. The brand's advertisements often feature prominent fashion icons and evoke a luxurious lifestyle.

2. **Nike**

    - **Visual Identity**: Nike's "swoosh" logo is among the most recognisable symbols globally. The simplicity and dynamic design of the logo convey movement and athletic excellence. Nike's bold, vibrant colours and modern typography further reinforce its identity.
    - **Brand Voice and Values**: Nike's brand voice is motivational and empowering, encouraging consumers to push their limits. The core values include innovation, performance, and inspiration.

- **Emotional Connection**: Nike leverages powerful storytelling through campaigns like "Just Do It," which resonates emotionally with athletes and non-athletes alike. Endorsements from top athletes and social causes support this emotional appeal.

3. **Patagonia**

   - **Visual Identity**: Patagonia's visual identity features a simple, rugged logo that reflects its commitment to outdoor adventure and environmental activism. Earth tones and natural imagery are consistent elements in its branding.
   - **Brand Voice and Values**: The brand voice is authentic and responsible, aligning with its values of sustainability, environmental stewardship, and quality.
   - **Emotional Connection**: Patagonia's firm stance on environmental issues and transparency creates a deep emotional bond with its consumers, who share similar values. Campaigns like "Don't Buy This Jacket" challenge consumerism and promote sustainability.

Key Lessons and Actionable Insights

1. **Consistency is Key**

   - The consistent use of visual elements (logo, colour palette, typography) across all touchpoints ensures that the brand is instantly recognisable.
   - **An example is** Chanel's unwavering use of its monochromatic palette and iconic logo in all its products and marketing materials.

2. **Emotional Storytelling**

   - Leveraging storytelling that resonates with the audience on an emotional level can significantly boost brand loyalty and engagement.

- **Example**: Nike's "Just Do It" campaigns inspire and motivate a broad audience, creating a strong emotional connection.

3. **Aligning with Core Values**

   - A brand's values should permeate every aspect of its identity, from visual design to communication. Brands that authentically live their values gain trust and loyalty.
   - **Example**: Patagonia's commitment to environmental causes is evident in its products, marketing, and corporate practices. This commitment has built a loyal customer base that shares these values.

4. **Adaptability and Evolution**

   - Brands must adapt to changing market trends and consumer feedback while maintaining their core identity. Regularly refreshing visual elements and messaging keeps the brand relevant.
   - **Example**: Burberry's rebranding efforts have modernised its image while preserving its heritage, aligning with contemporary consumer expectations.

Chapter 7

Product Manager as the CEO of the Product

"The Role of the Product Manager in the Success of the Brand"

The product manager's role in the fashion industry is pivotal to a brand's success. Often likened to an orchestra conductor, the product manager harmonises various functions—Research, Competition study, Design, Development/Sourcing/Production, Marketing, and sales—ensuring that each part works in concert to deliver products that resonate with consumers. This chapter delves into the multifaceted responsibilities of product managers, their impact on brand success, and the skills required to excel in this role.

Purpose and Importance of Product Management

Product management in fashion involves overseeing a product's entire lifecycle, from initial concept to final sale. This process requires a deep understanding of market trends, consumer behaviour, and the competitive landscape. A product manager's ability to navigate these complexities determines the brand's ability to innovate, meet market demands, and maintain a competitive edge.

Effective product management can significantly enhance a brand's competitiveness and profitability. According to a report by McKinsey, companies with strong product management practices see a 30% higher success rate in product launches.[28] Additionally, a survey by Pragmatic Institute found that 81% of product managers report a significant impact on their company's revenue growth[29].

Nike's Innovative Product Management

Nike exemplifies effective product management through its commitment to innovation and cross-functional collaboration. Its product managers lead brainstorming sessions, validate concepts with market research, and oversee the design and production phases. This collaborative approach has created iconic products like the Air Max series, which meet and often set market trends.

Key Responsibilities of a Product Manager

The product manager's role is diverse and dynamic. Key responsibilities include:

1. **Product Development**
2. **Market Research**
3. **Trend Analysis**
4. **Coordination and Collaboration**
5. **Go-to-Market Strategy (GTM)**
6. **Post-Launch Evaluation**

1. Product Development

Guiding the creation of new products, ensuring they align with market needs and brand identity.

---

28 A report by **McKinsey** titled **"What Separates Top Product Managers from the Rest of the Pack"**

29 Comes from the **Pragmatic Institute's Annual Product Management and Marketing Survey.**

Overseeing the entire process of bringing a product from concept to reality.

Collaborating with designers to ensure the product aligns with the brand's vision and market trends.

Example: At Nike, product managers lead the development of new footwear designs, working closely with designers and engineers to create innovative products like the Air Max series.

From **Sketch to Sample: A Closer Look at Product Development**

The design stage is one of the most critical stages of product development in fashion. It is where the fashion designer's creative vision comes to life.

The design process starts with a sketch. Fashion designers use sketches to develop ideas and communicate their designs to others. Once the sketch is complete, the designer creates a tech pack, a detailed document with design specifications such as materials, dimensions, and colours.

Next, the pattern-making process begins. This involves creating a template to cut the fabric for the garment. This stage requires technical expertise and attention to detail to ensure the garment fits correctly.

Once the pattern is complete, a prototype is made. The prototype is the first sample of the garment, created to test the design and fit. Fit testing is critical to product development, ensuring the garment fits properly and meets quality standards.

After the prototype is approved, the final samples are produced. These samples, such as photoshoots and fashion shows, are used for promotional purposes and are the basis for production.

5 Stages of the Fashion Product Development Process

Designing Concepts

The fashion development process starts with an idea. Fashion designers take the first step to turn their ideas into reality by crafting concept sketches of the design.

Ideas for the sketch may be drawn from mood boards, which inspire the product. The head of design usually starts a concept with a paper sketch, which is then handed off to other designers.

Designers brainstorm ideas to enhance the initial sketches and decide on specifications such as colours, patterns, accessories, and fabrics.

After creating a basic outline, the design may circulate, gathering approval from team members. It then moves on to a technical designer who delves deeper into the details and transforms it into a more workable sketch.

Technical designers craft their sketches to communicate the details of the fabric to the manufacturers. They highlight measurements, trim placement, seam line location, and other valuable information, making the sketch more practical.

The end piece is a technical sketch or a *fashion flat,* a two-dimensional representation of the finished garment made with software like AutoCAD or Adobe Illustrator.

Preparing Tech Packs

A tech pack is a detailed document that includes instructions for a supplier or manufacturer on making a specific piece of clothing. Suppliers don't take product orders without a tech pack because they require guidance on what's expected of them and how to deliver that product.

Creating a comprehensive tech pack will ensure the manufacturing unit has the key information to fulfil the product requirements. When creating your tech packs, make sure to include the following information:

Technical drawings of the garment

A visual mock-up of the finished garment

Size charts with appropriate grades

Spec sheet with real life examples

Placement of tags and labels

Assigning different grades to the garment can become advanced in the later stage of the production process, but including sizes for XS, S, M, L, XL, etc. is a good starting point for manufacturing.

Creating Samples

After gfinalising your designs, you'll create the first few samples of your garment. These samples will test how the product will look in real life. In this stage, there are two types of samples: proto samples and fit samples.

Proto samples are made from stock materials and colours. Their primary purpose is to visually represent your fashion design without going into too much detail. These samples are then tested to pinpoint any errors and make adjustments that assist in creating the fit sample.

The fit sample is a refined sample made from the correct measurements and the right fit after receiving feedback on the proto sample. It is then tested to eliminate any final errors.

Consistency is key in this stage. Make sure to use a model with a consistent sample, as the fit sample needs to have the correct fit and measurements. This stage is to fine-tune the fabric before sending it to batch production. Take your time with this; making multiple copies of the wrong fabric can waste time, material, and money.

You should also use the correct fabric instead of the stock fabric to create the prototype samples. Some fabrics may differ in tension, fitting, and draping, which can cause inconsistencies in the final design.

Other than the look of the garment, you need to see whether the mass production of the garment fits within your organisational capability. Consider the following factors:

Time sensitivity: Can the production process create the product within a set timeframe? Consider the difficulty and complexity of making the finished product and eliminate products you think will be less productive.

Price Point—How much will you market the product at? Are you looking to maximise profits or build strong brand recognition? Check to see if your price point makes sense for the clothing style and your customer base.

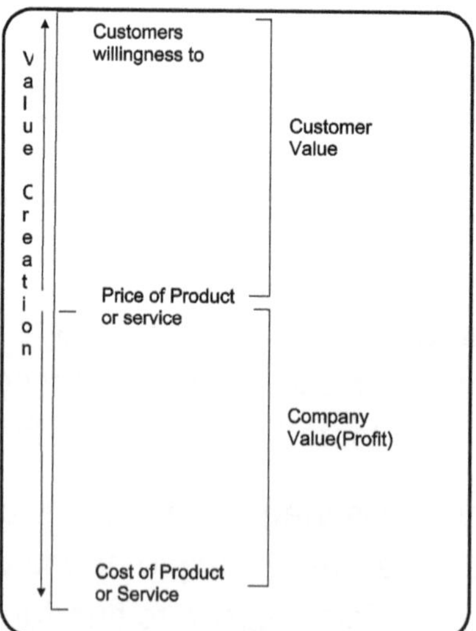

Expenses—How much would it cost you to create the product? Calculate your labour, fabric, and hardware/software costs and see if they align with your price points.

After completing these tests, choose your final sample and forward it to the manufacturer to give them the go-ahead to start production.

With finalised designs, tech packs, and fabric choices, the garment production process begins, encompassing phases like pre-production, cutting & sewing, quality checks, and final delivery. Start by contacting manufacturers for quotes and exploring options like production packages. Pre-sales can help estimate production quantities, minimising risks. Incorporate grading in patterns for size variations (S, M, L, XL), ensuring precise measurements are sent to manufacturers. Approve pre-production samples after thorough testing and feedback to guarantee quality.

Quality Control

Implement a multi-phase quality control process, checking fabrics for defects such as shade variations, uneven dyeing, or measurement issues during production and before packaging. This ensures market-ready products and fosters trustworthy supplier relationships.

PLM Software in Fashion

Fashion PLM (Product Lifecycle Management) software modernises inventory and production processes, replacing manual methods that are prone to errors. PLM centralises product data, streamlines workflows, and enhances collaboration between product developers, buyers, and suppliers. Accessible PLM tools, such as Infor Fashion PLM, help manage specifications, approvals, sample tracking, and development progress efficiently, making them an essential asset for established brands and startups.

2. Market Research and Trend Analysis

Market research and trend analysis are crucial components of product management in the fashion industry. They provide insights into consumer behaviour, market trends, and competitive landscapes, enabling fashion brands to make informed decisions and stay ahead of the curve. Here's a detailed explanation of these processes, including specific details, examples, statistics, charts, and survey results.

1. Understanding Market Research

Market research involves gathering and analysing data about consumers, competitors, and market conditions to inform business decisions. It helps fashion brands understand their target audience, identify market opportunities, and develop effective marketing strategies.

- **Surveys and Questionnaires**: Collecting data directly from consumers to understand their preferences, needs, and buying behaviours.
- **Focus Groups**: Conducting discussions with a small group of target customers to gain deeper insights into their opinions and preferences.
- **Competitive Analysis**: Analysing competitors' strategies, strengths, and weaknesses to identify market gaps and opportunities.
- **Sales Data Analysis**: Reviewing historical sales data to identify trends, patterns, and areas for improvement.

Example: Zara conducts extensive market research to understand consumer preferences and trends, allowing it to quickly adapt its product offerings to changing market demands.

2. Conducting Trend Analysis

Trend analysis involves identifying and predicting emerging trends in the fashion industry. It helps brands stay relevant and innovative by aligning their products with the latest styles, colours, and consumer preferences.

- **Fashion Shows and Trade Shows**: Attending events to observe the latest trends and gather insights from industry experts.
- **Social Media Monitoring**: Tracking popular hashtags, influencers, and consumer posts to identify emerging trends.
- **Fashion Publications and Reports**: Reviewing industry reports, magazines, and blogs to stay updated on the latest trends.
- **Consumer Behaviour Analysis**: Studying consumer purchasing patterns and preferences to predict future trends.

3. Integrating Market Research and Trend Analysis

Combining market research and trend analysis allows fashion brands to develop products that meet consumer demands and anticipate future trends. This integrated approach ensures that brands remain competitive and innovative.

- **Data Integration**: Combining market research and trend analysis data to understand the market comprehensively.
- **Collaborative Workshops**: Bringing together cross-functional teams to brainstorm and develop product concepts based on research insights.
- **Prototyping and Testing**: Creating prototypes and conducting consumer tests to validate product concepts and refine designs.
- **Strategic Planning**: Developing marketing and sales strategies based on research and trend insights to maximise product success.

H&M uses a combination of market research and trend analysis to develop its seasonal collections, ensuring that they align with consumer preferences and emerging trends.

Market research and trend analysis are essential for fashion brands aiming to start, scale, and stand out in the competitive fashion world. By understanding consumer preferences, identifying market opportunities, and predicting emerging trends, brands can develop products that resonate with their target audience and drive business success. Integrating these processes into product management ensures that brands remain innovative, relevant, and competitive in the ever-evolving fashion industry.

4. Collaboration: Working closely with design, marketing, and sales teams to ensure cohesive strategies and successful product launches.

Ensuring alignment of goals and seamless communication between departments.

Example: Adidas coordinates between its design and marketing teams to launch new collections effectively, ensuring that every team is aligned with the product vision.

Cross-functional collaboration—encompassing design, marketing, sales, and production—is essential for aligning goals and streamlining workflows. Brands like Adidas highlight this synergy by synchronising design and marketing efforts. Product managers rely on project management tools like Trello and Asana to track milestones and enhance productivity. Research shows that these platforms can improve team efficiency by up to 25%.

---

5. Go-to-Market Strategy (GTM)

A robust go-to-market strategy ensures a successful product launch. This includes market positioning, pricing strategies, and influencer partnerships. Glossier excels in leveraging social media influencers, while Warby Parker's online-offline marketing mix sets a high standard for launch effectiveness.

Developing a Go-to-Market Plan

A go-to-market plan outlines the steps for launching and marketing a product. It includes market positioning, marketing strategy, and sales tactics.

1. **Market Positioning**

   Market positioning involves defining how a product fits in the market and how it differentiates from competitors.

   Identifying the target audience and their preferences.

   Analysing competitors to find gaps and opportunities.

   Crafting a unique value proposition that highlights the product's benefits.

2. **Marketing Strategy**

   A marketing strategy outlines how to promote the product to the target audience effectively.

   Selecting the proper marketing channels (e.g. social media, email, influencer marketing).

   Creating compelling content and promotional materials.

   Planning marketing campaigns to generate buzz and drive traffic.

3. **Sales Tactics**

   Sales tactics involve the methods and techniques used to sell the product.

   Training the sales team on product features and benefits.

   Offering incentives and promotions to encourage sales.

   Using data-driven approaches to identify and target potential customers.

Example: Apple's sales team is well-trained in the features and benefits of new products, which helps them effectively sell and upsell products to customers.

Pricing and Promotion

Pricing and promotion strategies are crucial for driving sales and establishing the product in the market. These strategies should align with the overall go-to-market plan and target audience.

Strategies

1. **Competitive Pricing**:

   Setting prices based on competitors' pricing and market conditions. Conducting competitive analysis to understand market pricing. Determining price points that offer value while maintaining profitability. Adjusting prices based on market demand and competitor actions.

2. **Promotional Campaigns**: Creating and executing marketing campaigns to promote the product and drive sales.

   Designing promotional materials and advertisements.

   Planning and executing marketing campaigns across multiple channels.

   Offering limited-time discounts and special offers to create urgency.

3. **Influencer Partnerships**: Collaborating with influencers to promote the product to their followers.

   Identifying influencers whose audience aligns with the target market.

   Developing partnerships and creating sponsored content.

   Measuring the impact of influencer campaigns on brand awareness and sales.

- A survey by Influencer Marketing Hub found that 89% of marketers believe that influencer marketing provides a higher ROI than other marketing channels.[30]
- The Competitive Pricing Study by PwC revealed that 64% of consumers are influenced by price when purchasing, emphasising the importance of competitive pricing strategies.[31]

A successful product launch and go-to-market strategy is critical for the success of any fashion brand. By developing a comprehensive go-to-market plan that includes market positioning, marketing strategy, and sales tactics, and implementing effective pricing and promotion strategies, brands can ensure that their products reach the right audience, create a buzz, and achieve desired sales targets. Integrating these strategies into product management ensures that fashion brands remain competitive, innovative, and responsive to market demands.

---

6. Post-Launch Evaluation: Analysing product performance through metrics such as sales figures, customer feedback, and return rates.

Gathering insights to inform future product developments and improvements.

Example: Patagonia uses post-launch metrics to refine and improve its products, ensuring continuous improvement based on customer feedback.

30 from the **Influencer Marketing Hub's State of Influencer Marketing 2024 Benchmark Report**.

31 from **PwC's Global Consumer Insights Pulse Survey** conducted in June 2023

Effective product management is the cornerstone of innovation in fashion brands like Nike, where cross-functional collaboration fuels creativity. At Nike, product managers play a pivotal role in every stage of the product life cycle—from ideation and concept validation through design, production, and market launch. This approach has birthed iconic products like the Air Max series that shape market trends.

Post-launch Evaluation and Improvement are crucial steps in the product life cycle that ensure ongoing product success and brand growth. By analysing performance metrics and adapting to feedback and market changes, fashion brands can refine their products, enhance customer satisfaction, and maintain a competitive edge.

Performance Metrics

Performance metrics are essential for assessing the success of a product after its launch. These metrics provide valuable insights into how the product performs in the market and highlight areas for improvement.

Key Metrics

1. **Sales Figures**

   Sales figures indicate the number of units sold and the revenue generated by the product.

   Tracking daily, weekly and monthly sales data.

   Comparing sales performance against initial projections and targets.

2. **Customer Feedback**

   Customer feedback involves collecting and analysing opinions and experiences from customers who have purchased and used the product.

Conducting surveys and collecting reviews from customers.

Monitoring social media and online reviews for customer sentiments.

Glossier uses customer feedback from social media and its website to understand how well its products are received and to make necessary adjustments.

3. **Return Rates**

   Return rates measure the percentage of products returned by customers after purchase.

   Analysing return data to identify common reasons for returns.

   Investigating quality issues or customer dissatisfaction that led to returns.

   According to a Gartner report, companies that effectively monitor and analyse performance metrics post-launch achieve a 15-20% improvement in customer satisfaction and product success.

Continuous Improvement

Continuous improvement involves adapting to feedback and market changes to enhance product quality, performance, and customer satisfaction. This iterative process ensures that products remain competitive and relevant in the market.

1. **Adapting to Feedback**

   Implementing changes based on customer feedback to address issues and improve the product.

   Regularly reviewing feedback to identify trends and areas for improvement.

2. **Responding to Market Changes**

   Keeping abreast of market trends and competitor actions to adjust strategies accordingly.

Innovating and updating products to meet changing consumer preferences and market demands.

- A survey by Deloitte found that 72% of companies with continuous improvement processes experience higher customer satisfaction and loyalty.[32]

Post-launch evaluation and continuous improvement are essential for the ongoing success of fashion products. By effectively tracking performance metrics such as sales figures, customer feedback, and return rates, brands can gain valuable insights into their product performance. Adapting to feedback and market changes ensures that products remain competitive, meet customer expectations, and drive business growth. Integrating these practices into product management allows fashion brands to scale, innovate, and stand out in the competitive fashion world.

Coordination and collaboration are essential for effective product management in the fashion industry. A cross-functional partnership ensures that the goals of design, marketing, sales, and production teams are aligned, enhancing communication and streamlining processes. Supported by tools like Gantt charts and project management software, project management skills help product managers keep track of timelines, milestones, and deliverables. By mastering these aspects, fashion brands can improve efficiency, foster innovation, and successfully bring new products to market.

A product's lifecycle begins with ideation and concept development. It then progresses through design, prototyping, production, and quality control. The following steps involve crafting a marketing and

32 from **Deloitte's 2024 Global Consumer Insights Pulse Survey**.

sales strategy, launching the product, and managing distribution. Finally, post-launch analytics and continuous improvement are essential for ongoing success and refinement.

Product Lifecycle Management

Outline the stages from conception to launch, including development, marketing, sales, and post-launch analysis.

The product life cycle in fashion is a comprehensive process that involves several critical stages, from the initial concept to the post-launch evaluation. Each stage requires meticulous planning, collaboration, and execution to ensure the product meets market demands and contributes to the brand's success. Here's a detailed look at each stage of the product life cycle:

1. Ideation and Concept Development

This initial stage involves brainstorming and generating new product ideas. It is crucial to align these ideas with market trends, brand identity, and consumer preferences.

- Brainstorming sessions with cross-functional teams.
- Market research to identify gaps and opportunities.
- Concept validation through customer feedback and focus groups.

2. Design and Prototyping

Once the concept is finalised, the design and prototyping stage begins. This involves creating initial designs, developing prototypes, and refining them based on feedback.

- Sketching initial designs and creating digital renderings.
- Developing physical prototypes using advanced technologies like 3D printing.
- Iterative testing and refining prototypes.

3. Production and Quality Control

This stage focuses on scaling the production of the finalised design while maintaining high-quality. It involves selecting materials, coordinating with manufacturers, and implementing quality assurance measures.

- Selecting high-quality materials and suppliers.
- Coordinating with manufacturers to ensure efficient production.
- Conducting quality checks at various stages of production.

4. Marketing and Sales Strategy

A successful product launch requires a well-coordinated marketing and sales strategy. This involves positioning the product in the market, creating promotional campaigns, and preparing the sales team.

- Developing a go-to-market strategy that includes market positioning and target audience.
- Creating marketing campaigns that leverage various channels such as social media, influencers, and traditional media.
- Training the sales team on product features and benefits.

A report by McKinsey highlights that well-executed product launches can increase sales by 20-30%.

5. Product Launch and Distribution

This stage involves the official introduction of the product to the market. It includes logistics planning, distribution, and monitoring initial sales performance.

- Planning logistics to ensure timely delivery to stores and online platforms.

- Coordinating with distribution partners to maximise product availability.
- Monitoring initial sales performance to adjust strategies if needed.

Example: Apple's product launches are meticulously planned, with synchronised global distribution ensuring that new products are simultaneously available in stores and online.

6. Post-Launch Analysis and Continuous Improvement

After launching the product, it is essential to analyse its performance and gather feedback to inform future developments. This stage evaluates sales data, customer feedback, and return rates.

- Analysing sales data to measure product performance against targets.
- Collecting and reviewing customer feedback through surveys and reviews.
- Monitoring return rates to identify any quality or satisfaction issues.

Implementing improvements based on the analysis to enhance future products.

Understanding the product life cycle in fashion involves recognising the importance of each stage, from conception to post-launch analysis. Effective product management ensures that each stage is meticulously planned and executed, resulting in innovative products that meet market demands and contribute to the brand's success. By mastering these stages, fashion brands can stay competitive, creative, and responsive to consumer needs.

Key Takeaways from the Chapter:

1. Central Role of the Product Manager

- Fashion product managers act as orchestrators, harmonising diverse functions such as research, design, sourcing, production, marketing, and sales to deliver successful products.
- Their ability to align these areas determines a brand's capacity to innovate, meet market demands, and maintain a competitive edge.

2. Purpose and Impact of Product Management

- Product management oversees the entire product lifecycle, from concept to sale.
- Effective practices significantly improve competitiveness and profitability; for instance, strong product management can lead to a 30% higher success rate in product launches (McKinsey).

3. Key Responsibilities of a Product Manager

- **Product Development:** Ensuring products align with market needs and brand identity.
- **Market Research & Trend Analysis:** Using insights to anticipate consumer preferences and stay ahead of trends.
- **Coordination & Collaboration:** Cross-functional teamwork to align goals across departments.
- **Go-to-Market Strategy:** Crafting a robust launch plan, including market positioning, pricing, and promotional efforts.
- **Post-Launch Evaluation:** Monitoring metrics like sales, customer feedback, and returns to refine future products.

4. Product Development Process

- From sketches to prototypes, product managers guide the transformation of ideas into tangible products.

- Tools like tech packs and PLM software ensure efficient and error-free production.
- Quality control and consistency during the sampling and production phases are essential to minimise risks and optimise resources.

5. Leveraging Tools and Strategies

- Modern tools like PLM software streamline workflows and centralise product data.
- Project management platforms like Trello and Asana enhance efficiency and alignment, improving team productivity by up to 25%.

6. Strategic Market Positioning

- A clear go-to-market strategy includes defining target audiences, differentiating products, and leveraging influencers and promotional campaigns.
- Competitive pricing and innovative marketing tactics, such as Warby Parker's online-offline model, ensure successful launches.

7. Continuous Improvement

- Post-launch metrics such as sales figures, customer feedback, and return rates inform iterative improvements.
- Adapting to feedback and responding to market changes drives sustained relevance and consumer satisfaction.

8. Importance of Collaboration

- Cross-functional partnerships between design, marketing, and sales teams streamline workflows and foster innovation.
- Effective collaboration ensures cohesive strategies and seamless product launches.

9. Key Skills for Success

- Market insight, strategic planning, technical expertise in product development, and effective communication.

By mastering these elements, product managers drive product success and contribute significantly to the brand's overall growth and market leadership.

Product Lifecycle in Fashion

1. **Holistic Approach to Product Lifecycle**
   - The product lifecycle is a comprehensive process from ideation to post-launch analysis. It requires seamless integration of planning, collaboration, and execution to meet market demands and drive brand success.

2. **Ideation and Concept Development**
   - Begin with brainstorming aligned with market trends, brand identity, and consumer needs.
   - Use market research and customer feedback for concept validation.

3. **Design and Prototyping**
   - Create initial designs and prototypes, incorporating technologies like 3D printing.
   - Engage in iterative testing to refine and perfect the design.

4. **Production and Quality Control**
   - Focus on material selection, supplier coordination, and stringent quality assurance.
   - Conduct quality checks throughout production to ensure high standards.

5. **Marketing and Sales Strategy**
   - Develop a robust go-to-market plan, leveraging diverse marketing channels such as social media, influencers, and traditional media.
   - Train the sales team for effective product positioning.
   - Effective launches can significantly boost sales, as highlighted by McKinsey's insights.

6. **Product Launch and Distribution**
   - Plan logistics for timely delivery across platforms and regions.
   - Monitor early sales performance to make necessary adjustments.
   - Example: Apple's synchronised global launches exemplify efficient planning.

7. **Post-Launch Analysis and Continuous Improvement**
   - Analyse sales data, customer feedback, and return rates to evaluate performance.
   - Use insights to refine future products and strategies.

8. **The Value of Execution and Feedback**
   - Each stage is critical in innovation, market responsiveness, and brand competitiveness.
   - Continuous improvement based on analysis ensures product relevance and consumer satisfaction.

By mastering each stage of the product lifecycle, fashion brands can create innovative, market-relevant products while maintaining their competitive edge.

Chapter 8

Laying Down Brand Launch Guidelines (Go-to-Market Plan)

Angle: "The Launch Formula – Beyond Big Budgets"

Launching a fashion brand is a thrilling yet intricate journey that requires meticulous planning and strategic execution. In the fiercely competitive fashion landscape, having a well-defined go-to-market (GTM) plan is crucial for cutting through the noise and capturing the attention of your target audience. This chapter is dedicated to guiding you through establishing comprehensive brand launch guidelines, ensuring your entry into the market is impactful and sustainable.

A GTM plan is more than just a launch strategy; it's a roadmap that defines how you will position your brand, engage with your audience, and achieve your business objectives. According to a report by CB Insights, 42% of startups fail because there is no market need for their product, underscoring the importance of thorough market research and strategic planning[33]. By leveraging data and insights, you can tailor your approach to meet your target demographic's needs and preferences, increasing your chances of success.

Consider the exemplary launch of Warby Parker, a brand that disrupted the eyewear industry with its direct-to-consumer model.

---

33 from a report by **CB Insights** titled **"The Top 12 Reasons Startups Fail."**

Warby Parker successfully captured a significant market share by understanding its market, positioning itself as a stylish yet affordable alternative, and using innovative marketing tactics. Its GTM plan strongly emphasised digital marketing, influencer partnerships, and a unique home try-on programme, resonating deeply with its audience and setting it apart from competitors.

This chapter will explore the key components of an effective GTM plan, including market analysis, brand positioning, marketing and sales strategies, and performance metrics. You'll learn how to identify your unique value proposition, craft compelling marketing messages, and leverage various channels to reach and engage your audience. Additionally, we will delve into the importance of adaptability, as market conditions and consumer behaviours are constantly evolving.

Through detailed explanations, real-world examples, and practical insights, this chapter will equip you with the tools and knowledge needed to launch your fashion brand successfully and stand out in the competitive fashion world. Whether you're a budding entrepreneur or an established brand looking to reinvent itself, this chapter will provide a robust foundation for your brand's journey to the market.

Launch Planning Essentials: Checklist for a Successful Launch

Launching a fashion brand is an intricate process that requires careful planning and execution. A well-organised launch plan serves as a roadmap, guiding you through the critical steps necessary to effectively introduce your brand to the market. Here's a comprehensive checklist to ensure a successful launch.

1. Market Research and Analysis

- Identify Target Audience: Understand your potential customers' preferences and buying behaviour. Gather insights using surveys, focus groups, and market reports.
- Competitive Analysis: Analyse your competitors to identify their strengths and weaknesses. Tools like SWOT analysis can help understand where your brand can differentiate itself.

2. Define Brand Positioning

- Unique Selling Proposition (USP): Clearly articulate what differentiates your brand. This could be based on quality, price, design, sustainability, or customer service.
- Brand Messaging: Develop key messages communicating your brand's value proposition to your target audience. Ensure consistency across all communication channels.

3. Product Development and Inventory Management

- Finalise product Line: Ensure that your product offerings are ready for launch. This includes completing design, production, and quality checks.
- Inventory Planning: Based on market research, estimate the demand and plan your inventory accordingly to avoid overstocking or stockouts.

4. Marketing and Promotion Strategy

- Digital Marketing: Plan your online presence through a robust website, social media profiles, and email marketing campaigns. According to HubSpot, 81% of shoppers conduct online research before purchasing, highlighting the importance of a strong digital presence.
- Influencer Partnerships: Collaborate with fashion influencers to expand your reach and build credibility. A study by Influencer Marketing Hub found that businesses make an average of $5.78 for every dollar spent on influencer marketing.
- Content Creation: Develop engaging content that showcases your products and tells your brand story. Use high-quality images, videos, and blog posts to attract and retain customers.

5. Sales and Distribution Channels

- E-commerce Platforms: Set up your online store on platforms like Shopify, WooCommerce, or BigCommerce. Ensure a seamless user experience and secure payment options.
- Physical Retail: If applicable, plan for pop-up shops, trunk shows, or partnerships with established retailers. This provides customers with a tangible experience of your brand.

6. Public Relations and Launch Events

- Press Releases: Write and distribute press releases to announce your brand launch to media outlets. This can generate buzz and attract media coverage.
- Launch Events: Organise a launch event or virtual unveiling to create excitement and give influencers, the media, and potential customers a first-hand experience of your brand.

7. Customer Engagement and Feedback

- Customer Service: Set up efficient customer service processes for inquiries, orders, and returns. Exceptional customer service can build trust and loyalty.
- Feedback Mechanisms: Implement systems to gather feedback from your initial customers. Use this information to make necessary adjustments and improvements.

8. Monitoring and Analytics

- Performance Metrics: Track key performance indicators (KPIs) such as website traffic, social media engagement, sales, and customer acquisition costs. Google Analytics and social media insights can provide valuable data.
- Adjust and Adapt: Be prepared to tweak your strategies based on performance data and market feedback. Continuous improvement is essential for long-term success.

Key Metrics for Launch Success

Metric	Target	Tool/Method
Website Traffic	Increase by 50% in the first 3 months	Google Analytics
Social Media Engagement	Achieve 10,000 followers in the first 6 months	Social media analytics
Customer Acquisition Cost	Reduce by 20% within the first year	Marketing budget analysis
Sales Growth	Double monthly sales by the end of the first year	E-commerce platform reports

This checklist ensures a thorough and strategic approach to launching your fashion brand. By paying attention to each component, you can position your brand for a successful market entry and build a strong foundation for growth.

Choosing the Right Channels: Digital, Retail, Pop-Ups, and Other Launch Platforms

Selecting the proper channels to launch your fashion brand is essential for effectively reaching your target audience and maximising your brand's impact. Each channel offers unique benefits and challenges; the right mix can significantly enhance your launch success.

1. Digital Channels

Digital channels are crucial for modern brand launches, offering vast reach and flexibility.

- **E-commerce Website**: Your e-commerce website serves as the central hub for your brand. It provides complete control over the customer experience, from browsing to purchasing. According to Statista, global e-commerce sales are expected to reach $6.38 trillion by 2024, highlighting the importance of having a strong online presence.
- **Social Media**: Platforms like Instagram, Facebook, TikTok, and Pinterest are invaluable for building brand awareness and engaging with your audience. Each platform has strengths; Instagram is great for visual storytelling, while TikTok excels with short, viral content. A report by Sprout Social found that 77% of consumers are more likely to buy from brands they follow on social media.
- **Email Marketing**: Email remains a powerful tool for direct communication with potential customers. Building an email list allows for personalised marketing and exclusive offers, driving higher engagement and conversions.
- **Influencer Marketing**: Collaborating with influencers can significantly boost your brand's visibility and credibility. Influencers have dedicated followers who trust their recommendations, making them powerful allies in your

launch strategy. A survey by Influencer Marketing Hub shows that businesses earn $5.78 for every dollar spent on influencer marketing.

2. Retail Channels

Physical retail provides a tangible experience for customers to interact with your brand.

- **Flagship Stores**: Establishing a flagship store in a prime location can create a strong brand presence. This space should reflect your brand's identity and offer an immersive shopping experience. Apple's flagship stores are prime examples, offering a seamless blend of retail and brand experience.
- **Department Stores and Boutiques**: Partnering with established retailers can expand your reach and tap into your customer base. Ensure that your brand aligns with the retailer's image and values for a cohesive partnership.

3. Pop-Up Shops

Pop-up shops are temporary retail spaces that create excitement and exclusivity around your brand.

- **Experiential Marketing**: Pop-ups offer a unique opportunity for experiential marketing, where customers can engage with your brand in a novel way. This can include interactive displays, exclusive product launches, and special events.
- **Market Testing**: Pop-ups allow you to test new markets and gather direct customer feedback without the commitment of a permanent retail space. According to Storefront, 80% of global retail companies consider experiential retail crucial to their business strategy.

4. Other Launch Platforms

- **Trunk Shows**: Hosting trunk shows lets you showcase your collection in an intimate setting. These events can be exclusive, invite-only, or open to the public, providing a personal touch and building relationships with customers.
- **Trade Shows and Fashion Weeks:** Participating in trade shows and fashion weeks can boost your brand's visibility and credibility within the industry. These events attract buyers, media, and influencers and provide valuable networking opportunities.
- **Warby Parker**: Warby Parker was successfully launched by combining a strong e-commerce presence with innovative pop-up shops. Their home try-on programme and engaging social media campaigns created a buzz, helping them capture a significant market share.
- **Glossier**: Glossier leveraged its digital platform and social media presence to build a loyal community before opening physical stores. Their pop-up shops in major cities created significant hype and demand, driving online and offline sales.

Channel	Strengths	Example
E-commerce Website	Full control over customer experience, broad reach	Glossier
Social Media	High engagement, visual storytelling	Warby Parker
Email Marketing	Personalized communication, high conversion rates	Various Brands
Influencer Marketing	Credibility and reach, strong ROI	Various Brands
Flagship Stores	Brand presence, immersive experience	Apple
Pop-Up Shops	Experiential marketing, market testing	Various Brands
Trunk Shows	Personal touch, relationship building	Various Brands
Trade Shows/Fashion Weeks	Industry visibility, networking opportunities	Various Brands

Choosing the right mix of launch channels is critical for reaching your target audience and creating a memorable brand experience. By leveraging the strengths of each channel and aligning them with your brand strategy, you can ensure a successful and impactful launch.

Building Pre-Launch Hype: Marketing Tactics to Create Anticipation

Creating buzz and excitement before launching your fashion brand is crucial for capturing attention and building a solid customer base from day one. Effective pre-launch marketing tactics can generate anticipation and ensure a successful entry into the market. Here's how to build pre-launch hype:

1. Teaser Campaigns

- **Sneak Peeks and Teasers**: Share glimpses of your upcoming products through social media posts, videos, and stories. This builds curiosity and excitement. Fashion brands like Gucci and Dior often release teaser videos showcasing snippets of their new collections.
- **Countdowns**: Implement countdowns on your website and social media platforms, highlighting the launch date. This creates a sense of urgency and anticipation among potential customers.

2. Influencer Collaborations

- **Influencer Partnerships**: Collaborate with fashion influencers to promote your brand before the official launch. Influencers can provide authentic endorsements and reach a large, engaged audience. Influencer Marketing Hub says influencer marketing can yield a 5.78 ROI for every dollar spent.[34]

---

34 from the **Influencer Marketing Hub's State of Influencer Marketing 2024 Benchmark Report**.

- **Unboxing Videos**: Send exclusive pre-launch products to influencers and encourage them to create unboxing videos. This generates excitement and provides social proof of your brand's quality.

3. Exclusive Pre-Launch Events

- **Virtual Launch Events**: Host a virtual launch event to introduce your brand to a broader audience. Use platforms like Instagram Live, YouTube, or Zoom to showcase your products, tell your brand story, and interact with potential customers.
- **VIP Previews**: Offer exclusive previews to select customers or influencers. This creates a sense of exclusivity and makes attendees feel unique and valued.

4. Social Media Campaigns

- **Hashtag Campaigns**: Create a unique, branded hashtag and encourage users to share content related to your brand. This helps build a community and increase brand visibility. For example, Calvin Klein's #MyCalvins campaign successfully engaged users and increased brand awareness.
- **Engaging Content**: Share behind-the-scenes content, design inspiration, and founder stories. Authentic and engaging content helps build a connection with your audience.

5. Email Marketing

- **Building an Email List**: Build an email list well before your launch. Offer incentives like exclusive discounts or early access to encourage sign-ups. According to HubSpot, email generates an average return of $42 for every dollar spent.

- **Pre-Launch Newsletters**: Send regular newsletters to keep your audience informed and excited about the upcoming launch. Include sneak peeks, product information, and launch details.

6. Partnerships and Collaborations

- **Strategic Partnerships**: Partner with complementary brands or local businesses to cross-promote your launch. This can help expand your reach and attract new customers.
- **Collaborative Events**: Co-host events or giveaways with other brands to create a buzz and attract a wider audience.

7. Early Access and Limited Editions

- **Early Access Offers**: Provide early access to your products for a limited number of customers or newsletter subscribers. This creates a sense of exclusivity and urgency.
- **Limited-Edition Products**: Launch limited-edition products to create a sense of scarcity and exclusivity. Limited time offers can drive quick sales and generate excitement.

8. Press Coverage and PR

- **Press Releases**: Distribute press releases to fashion magazines, blogs, and news outlets. Highlight your brand's unique aspects and explain why it stands out.
- **Media Outreach**: Reach out to fashion journalists and bloggers to secure coverage and reviews of your brand. Positive media coverage can significantly boost your brand's credibility and visibility.
- **Fenty Beauty**: Rihanna used a comprehensive pre-launch strategy, including teaser campaigns, influencer collaborations, and a major launch event. The brand generated massive hype and achieved $100 million in sales within its first 40 days.

- **Glossier**: Glossier built pre-launch hype by leveraging its blog readership, social media presence, and community engagement. The brand's approach included sneak peeks, influencer partnerships, and engaging content, leading to a successful launch.

Marketing Tactic	Effectiveness	Example Brand
Teaser Campaigns	High engagement and curiosity	Dior, Gucci
Influencer Collaborations	Strong ROI and credibility	Fenty Beauty
Exclusive Events	Increased sense of exclusivity	Glossier
Email Marketing	High ROI and direct communication	Various Brands
Social Media Campaigns	Community building and brand visibility	Calvin Klein

Building pre-launch hype creates anticipation and excitement, which translates into strong brand awareness and customer interest. You can ensure a successful and impactful launch for your fashion brand by leveraging these marketing tactics.

Key Takeaways: Laying Down Brand Launch Guidelines (Go-to-Market Plan)

1. **Strategic Go-to-Market (GTM) Planning**
   - A GTM plan is a roadmap for positioning your brand, engaging with your target audience, and achieving business goals.
   - Thorough market research ensures your brand addresses a genuine market need, reducing the risk of failure.

2. **Market Research and Analysis**
   - Identify your target audience using surveys, focus groups, and market reports.
   - Conduct a competitive analysis (e.g. SWOT) to pinpoint opportunities for differentiation.

3. **Define Brand Positioning**
   - Establish your Unique Selling Proposition (USP) based on factors like quality, price, sustainability, or innovation.
   - Develop a consistent brand messaging to convey your value proposition across channels.
4. **Product and Inventory Management**
   - Ensure products are launch-ready through rigorous quality checks.
   - Plan inventory levels based on market research to avoid shortages or excess stock.
5. **Effective Marketing and Promotion**
   - Build a strong digital presence through a website, social media, and email campaigns.
   - Leverage influencer partnerships for reach and credibility, yielding significant ROI.
   - Create engaging content (e.g. videos, images, and blogs) to attract and retain your audience.
6. **Launch Channels and Strategies**
   - Utilise e-commerce platforms for flexibility and scalability.
   - Consider physical retail through flagship stores, pop-up shops, or collaborations with established retailers.
   - For direct customer engagement, use experiential retail strategies, like pop-ups and trunk shows.
7. **Building Pre-Launch Hype**
   - Employ teaser campaigns, countdowns, and influencer collaborations to generate excitement.
   - Host exclusive events, VIP previews, or virtual launches to build anticipation.

- Create engaging social media campaigns using branded hashtags and behind-the-scenes content.

8. **Public Relations and Press Coverage**
   - Distribute press releases and secure media coverage to boost credibility.
   - Collaborate with journalists and fashion bloggers to highlight your brand's uniqueness.

9. **Monitoring and Adaptability**
   - Track performance metrics like website traffic, social media engagement, and sales.
   - Use data insights to refine strategies and respond to market feedback dynamically.

10. **Checklist for a Successful Launch**
    - Include steps such as conducting market research, defining positioning, preparing products, and planning distribution.
    - Use data-driven marketing, customer feedback, and performance analysis to ensure long-term success.

By following these guidelines and leveraging strategic planning, you can make a memorable market entry and establish a strong foundation for your brand's growth.

Part Three

SCALING

Chapter 9

The Art of Sourcing and Inventory Management

"Sourcing as Brand Building"

> *"In fashion, agility is the new luxury. Brands that adapt quickly don't just survive; they lead the way." – Adapted from McKinsey.*

Effective sourcing and inventory management are the cornerstones of building a sustainable and scalable brand in the dynamic and ever-evolving fashion industry. As fashion entrepreneurs strive to meet the demands of a competitive market, mastering the art of sourcing materials and managing inventory becomes crucial. These components not only influence the operational efficiency of a brand but also impact profitability, customer satisfaction, and overall market presence. This chapter delves into the intricate processes and strategies that underpin successful sourcing and inventory management, providing valuable insights and practical examples for fashion entrepreneurs.

Prioritise Speed and Adaptability

In the modern fashion industry, speed and adaptability are no longer luxuries but essential for survival and growth. Consumer preferences shift rapidly, trends evolve overnight, and external factors like economic shifts or global crises can instantly disrupt supply chains. To thrive in such a dynamic environment, fashion brands must be quick to respond and flexible in their approach.

Why Speed and Adaptability Matter

1. **Changing Consumer Behaviour:** Millennials and Gen Z demand instant gratification, with 40% of consumers expecting brands to launch new collections frequently.
2. **Shorter Trend Cycles:** Micro-trends rise and fall within months, requiring brands to act fast to capture their moment.
3. **Global Competition:** E-commerce and globalisation have made the market more competitive, putting pressure on brands to stand out quickly.

Fashion Industry Examples

1. **Zara**
    - Zara is a global leader in fast-fashion because of its agile supply chain. The brand can take a design from concept to store shelves in just two weeks, compared to the industry standard of six months.
    - This speed allows Zara to refresh collections frequently, ensuring stores always reflect current trends.
    - Speed empowers Zara to capture trends at their peak, minimising unsold inventory.
2. **H&M Conscious Collection**
    - H&M tests sustainable fabric innovations in small, limited-edition collections before rolling them out on a larger scale.
    - This adaptable approach allows them to experiment without overcommitting, reducing risk while promoting sustainability.

3. **Myntra (India)**
    - Myntra's "End of Reason Sale" uses AI to predict consumer demand in real-time, allowing the company to restock popular products quickly during sales events.
    - Their adaptability ensures customer satisfaction, leading to higher sales and reduced cart abandonment.

Statistics Supporting the Need for Speed

- 62% of fashion retailers say agility is critical for maintaining profitability in a competitive market.[35]
- A McKinsey report highlights that fashion brands with shorter production cycles grow revenues 50% faster than their slower counterparts[36].

How to Build Speed and Adaptability into Your Brand

1. Adopt Agile Design Processes: Work in short cycles to create, test, and refine products.

Inspired by software development methodologies, agile design processes offer a powerful way for fashion brands to maintain speed and adaptability in a highly dynamic market. In the fast-paced fashion industry, where consumer preferences shift rapidly and global trends evolve overnight, agility is not a luxury—it's a necessity.

---

35 from a report by **3DLOOK** titled **"11 Fashion Industry Challenges to Overcome in 2025."**

36 McKinsey report titled **"The State of Fashion 2024"**

Why Agile Design Matters

1. **Respond to Trends in Real-Time**: A McKinsey report highlights that brands embracing agile practices can reduce product development cycles by **30-50%**, enabling quicker responses to market demand.[37]
2. **Enhance Collaboration**: Agile encourages cross-functional teamwork, uniting design, production, and marketing teams to deliver cohesive results.
3. **Reduce Waste**: By focusing on iterative design and consumer feedback, brands can avoid overproduction and align with sustainable practices.

How to Implement Agile Design

1. **Iterative Design Cycles involve** Releasing small collections or prototypes and refining them based on feedback. For example, **Zara** launches new designs within **3-4 weeks** of spotting a trend using rapid prototyping.
2. **Customer Feedback Integration**: Platforms like Myntra's Style Studio in India leverage AI-driven insights and real-time customer preferences to inform design iterations.

- **H&M's Conscious Collection**: H&M piloted sustainable materials in small batches, gauged customer responses, and scaled up successful designs.
- **FabIndia**: The brand collaborates directly with artisans, incorporating their real-time input to refine product designs that appeal to domestic and global audiences.

---

37 from a McKinsey report titled **"Agile in the Consumer-Goods Industry: The Transformation of the Brand Manager"**

Statistics and Data

- According to a **Deloitte study**, agile fashion brands achieve **15% higher margins** by responding faster to consumer needs.[38]
- A survey by **BoF and McKinsey** found that **50% of fashion executives prioritise agility as a top strategy for growth.**[39]

A timeline comparison of traditional vs agile design cycles, showing shorter lead times for agile processes. [40]

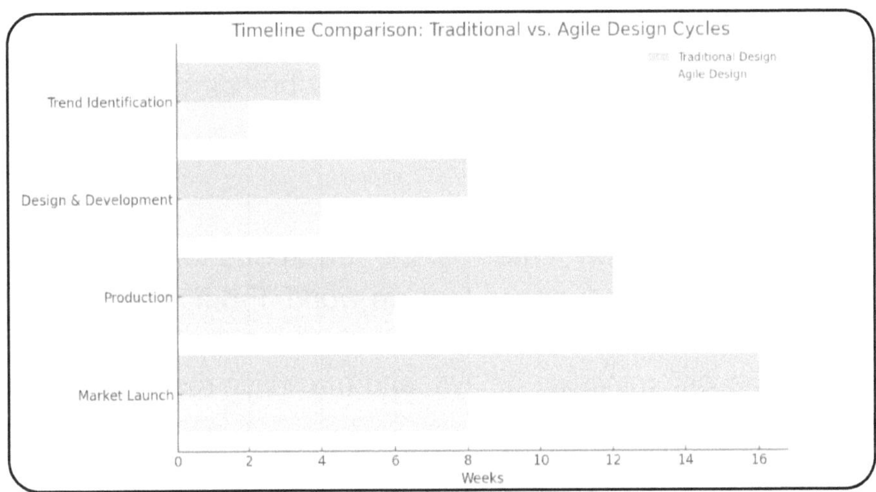

Agile design processes empower fashion brands to thrive in a world where speed and adaptability are key. By iterating quickly, engaging consumers, and refining products in real-time, brands

38 from a **Deloitte** study titled **"Global Powers of Luxury Goods 2022."**

39 from the **BoF-McKinsey State of Fashion 2024 Executive Survey**. You can find more details about this survey and its findings in the **"State of Fashion 2024"**

40 McKinsey report titled **"The State of Fashion 2024"**.

stay ahead of trends and build deeper connections with their audiences.

"Agility in design is not just about speed – it's about evolving with purpose, driven by the voice of your customer."

2. Streamline Supply Chains: Partner with manufacturers who can deliver quickly and adjust production based on demand.

In an industry as dynamic as fashion, where trends emerge and fade within weeks, the ability to adapt quickly and effectively is critical. Inspired by the tech industry's agile methodology, agile design processes enable fashion brands to meet consumer demands rapidly while maintaining high-quality and creativity. This approach focuses on flexibility, iterative improvements, and cross-functional collaboration, transforming how brands conceptualise, produce, and market their collections.

A streamlined supply chain is the backbone of speed and adaptability in the fast-paced fashion world. From raw materials to the final product, every link in the chain must function efficiently to reduce costs, minimise delays, and maximise responsiveness to market demands.

Core Elements of a Streamlined Supply Chain

1. **Real-Time Data Integration**

    - Brands use digital tools, such as ERP (Enterprise Resource Planning) and PLM (Product Lifecycle Management) systems, to track inventory, monitor shipments, and manage production timelines.

- Example: **Nike** employs predictive analytics to adjust inventory in real-time, reducing excess stock and ensuring fast replenishment.

2. **Local Sourcing and Nearshoring**
    - Instead of relying on distant suppliers, nearshoring shortens production lead times.
    - Example: **Arvind Ltd.** in India supplies fabrics to local brands like FabIndia, cutting transit time and fostering regional economic growth.

3. **Demand-Driven Production**
    - Adopting a "made-to-order" or "test-and-replenish" model ensures production meets actual consumer demand.
    - Example: **Shein** uses data from online searches and customer behaviour to produce only what sells, reducing waste.

Statistics Supporting Streamlining

- According to **McKinsey**, supply chain disruptions can cost brands up to **45% of their annual profits**, highlighting the need for efficiency.[41]
- A **Gartner survey** revealed that **65% of fashion brands** believe digitising their supply chain has reduced lead times by an average of **20%**.[42]

41 from a McKinsey report titled **"Future-proofing the Supply Chain"**.

42 McKinsey report titled **"State of Fashion Technology Report 2022"**

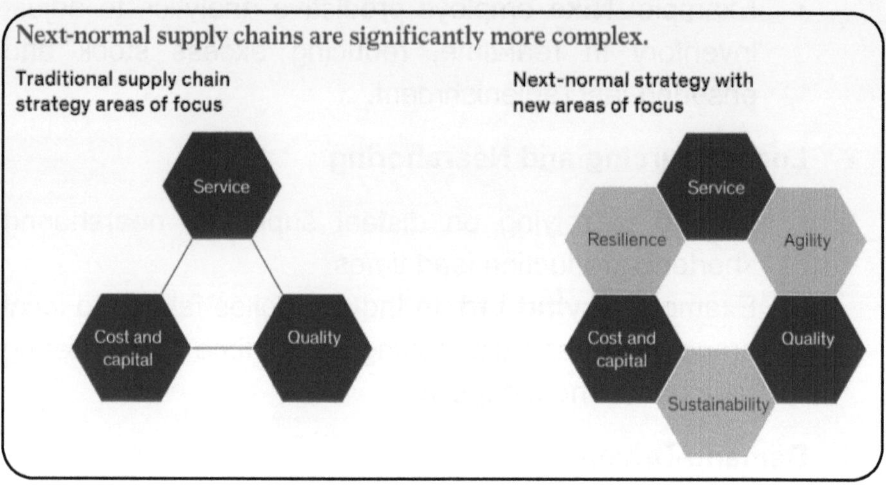

Indian Fashion Industry Examples

1. Myntra's Rapid Supply Chain Model: Myntra collaborates with domestic suppliers to ensure a two-week production cycle for their private labels.

2. Raymond: Streamlined vertical integration allows them to manage everything from fabric production to garment creation under one roof, enabling quick delivery.

Traditional vs Streamlined Supply Chains

Metric	Traditional Supply Chain	Streamlined Supply Chain
Lead Time	6–12 months	2–6 weeks
Inventory Holding Costs	High	Low
Responsiveness to Trends	Slow	Fast
Waste Generation	High	Low

Key Steps to Streamline Your Supply Chain

1. **Digitise Operations:** Use technologies like blockchain for transparency and AI for demand forecasting.
2. **Build Local Partnerships:** Collaborate with suppliers close to your target market to reduce shipping delays.
3. **Implement Lean Manufacturing:** Focus on reducing waste and improving process efficiency.

Streamlining your supply chain accelerates time to market and ensures resilience to disruptions. By embracing technology, fostering regional partnerships, and adopting lean methodologies, your brand can maintain speed and adaptability while remaining cost-effective.

> *"A fast, responsive supply chain is the silent powerhouse behind every successful fashion brand."*

3. Leverage Technology: Use AI to analyse trends, predict demand, and optimise inventory.

Technology is a game-changer in the fashion industry, enabling brands to adapt quickly, innovate effectively, and maintain a competitive edge. By integrating cutting-edge tools, fashion brands can enhance design, production, marketing, and customer engagement.

Key Areas Where Technology Enhances Speed and Adaptability

1. **AI-Powered Design**
   - Artificial intelligence helps designers predict trends, create virtual prototypes, and optimise collections based on market data.
   - **Example: Tommy Hilfiger** uses IBM's AI tools to analyse fashion trends, leading to more relevant designs with shorter turnaround times.

2. **3D Design and Virtual Sampling**
   - 3D modelling allows designers to visualise garments digitally, reducing the need for physical samples and accelerating approval.
   - **Example:** Indian brand **House of Anita Dongre** adopted 3D tools to speed up the sampling phase, cutting lead times by over **30%**.

3. **Smart Manufacturing with IoT**
   - Internet of Things (IoT) devices track production in real-time, ensuring efficiency and minimising delays.
   - **Example: Raymond** uses IoT in its factories to monitor processes, reducing downtime and improving productivity. Blue Kaktus provides a platform where the supply chain can be integrated on one page, and the real-time status of the orders and developments can be tracked.

4. **Augmented Reality (AR) in Marketing**
   - AR lets consumers try-on clothes virtually, boosting online sales and reducing returns.
   - **Example:** Myntra introduced AR-based virtual try-ons during their sale season, leading to a **20% increase in conversion rates**.

5. **Blockchain for Transparency**
   - Blockchain ensures traceability in the supply chain, building trust with consumers.
   - **Example: Levi's** employs blockchain to certify sustainable practices, enhancing their brand's credibility.

Technology Adoption in the Fashion Industry

Technology	Function	Impact
AI Design Tools	Predict trends, optimize designs	Shortens design phases by **40%**
3D Prototyping	Create virtual samples	Reduces sample costs by **60%**
IoT in Manufacturing	Real-time production tracking	Cuts downtime by **25%**
AR for Consumer Experience	Virtual try-ons	Increases online sales by **20%**
Blockchain	Supply chain transparency	Enhances trust and loyalty

---

Steps to Leverage Technology

1. **Assess Your Needs:** Identify the pain points in your processes and prioritise tech solutions accordingly.
2. **Invest in Scalable Tools:** Choose platforms and tools that can grow with your brand.
3. **Train Your Team:** Equip employees with the skills to effectively integrate and utilise new technologies.

Conclusion

Technology is no longer optional in fashion; it is essential. By leveraging tools like AI, AR, IoT, and blockchain, brands can increase efficiency, enhance customer experiences, and stay ahead of the competition. Technology provides the agility and innovation necessary to succeed in a rapidly changing market.

> *"Technology is the fabric that weaves creativity and speed into the future of fashion."*

Criteria for Selecting Suppliers

Criteria	Importance	Examples/Statistics
Quality	Ensures product meets standards and customer expectations	86% of consumers are willing to pay more for quality (Retail Dive)
Cost	Impacts pricing strategy and competitiveness	Primark's low-cost sourcing model
Reliability	Ensures timely delivery and consistent supply	Lululemon's reliable supply chain
Sustainability	Aligns with consumer demand for ethical products	66% of consumers willing to pay more for sustainable products (Nielsen)

Case Study: Patagonia's Sustainable Sourcing

Patagonia is a leading example of a brand successfully integrating sustainability into its sourcing practices. The brand sources materials from suppliers who meet rigorous environmental and social standards, such as using recycled polyester and organic cotton. This commitment reduces the ecological impact and resonates with Patagonia's customer base, which values sustainability. Its transparent sourcing practices have built strong customer loyalty and set a benchmark for other brands in the industry.

Understanding sourcing in the fashion industry involves a strategic approach to selecting and managing suppliers, balancing cost and quality, and adhering to ethical standards. By prioritising these aspects, fashion brands can build a resilient supply chain that supports their growth and aligns with consumer expectations.

3. Supplier Selection and Relationship Management

Selecting the right suppliers and building strong, collaborative relationships with them is paramount to the success of your fashion brand. This process involves evaluating potential suppliers based on various criteria and ensuring they align with your brand's quality, cost, reliability, and sustainability goals. Effective supplier relationship management (SRM) goes beyond mere transactions; it requires nurturing long-term partnerships to drive innovation, efficiency, and a competitive advantage.

Criteria for Selecting Suppliers

1. **Quality**: Ensuring the supplier consistently delivers products that meet your quality standards. High-quality materials are essential for maintaining brand reputation and customer satisfaction. Lululemon's meticulous selection of suppliers for its technical fabrics ensures that the end products meet stringent performance and quality standards.
2. **Cost**: Procuring materials at competitive prices to maintain profitability. While cost is a crucial factor, it should not come at the expense of quality or ethical considerations. Primark's sourcing strategy from low-cost suppliers enables it to offer competitively priced products while maintaining profitability.
3. **Reliability** is the ability of a supplier to deliver goods on time and consistently meet production schedules. Reliable suppliers help prevent production delays and stockouts, ensuring a steady supply of products. H&M's reliable supplier network allows it to restock stores and meet customer demand quickly without significant delays.

4. **Sustainability**: Ensuring that suppliers adhere to ethical labour practices and environmental standards. Sustainable sourcing aligns with growing consumer demand for ethically produced goods and enhances brand reputation. Patagonia's commitment to sustainability involves working with suppliers who meet rigorous environmental and social standards.

Building Strong Supplier Relationships

- **Communication**: Maintaining clear, open, and frequent communication with suppliers. Effective communication helps resolve issues quickly, align expectations, and foster collaboration. Nike's transparent communication with suppliers ensures mutual understanding and smooth operations, helping them maintain a robust supply chain.
- **Collaboration**: Working closely with suppliers to improve processes, innovate, and achieve mutual goals. Collaboration can lead to innovations in product development, cost reductions, and enhanced quality. Zara collaborates with its suppliers to develop new fabrics and designs, allowing for rapid adaptation to fashion trends.
- **Trust and Mutual Benefit**: Building trust-based relationships that benefit both parties. Trust fosters long-term partnerships, loyalty, and willingness to invest in joint initiatives. Patagonia's long-term relationships with key suppliers are based on trust and shared values, leading to greater collaboration and mutual success.

Strategies for Effective Supplier Relationship Management (SRM)

1. **Performance Monitoring**
    - Regularly assessing supplier performance based on key metrics such as quality, delivery times, and compliance.

- Utilise performance scorecards and regular audits to track and evaluate supplier performance.
- Apple conducts regular audits and assessments of its suppliers to ensure compliance with quality and ethical standards.

2. **Incentivising Excellence**

   - Providing incentives for suppliers to exceed performance expectations.
   - Incentives can motivate suppliers to maintain high standards and innovate.
   - Toyota's supplier reward programmes recognise and reward suppliers who demonstrate exceptional performance and innovation.

3. **Conflict Resolution**

   - Establishing clear procedures for resolving disputes and issues with suppliers.
   - Effective conflict resolution mechanisms help maintain healthy supplier relationships and avoid disruptions.
   - Uniqlo's conflict resolution process involves regular meetings and open dialogue with suppliers to address and resolve issues promptly.

4. **Joint Development Initiatives**

   - Engaging in joint development projects with suppliers to create new products or improve processes.
   - Joint initiatives can lead to innovative solutions and competitive advantages.
   - Adidas collaborates with suppliers on R&D projects to develop new materials and sustainable production methods.

In conclusion, supplier selection and relationship management are pivotal for ensuring your fashion brand can reliably and sustainably deliver high-quality products. You can build a resilient supply chain that supports your brand's growth and success by prioritising quality, cost, reliability, and sustainability in supplier selection and fostering strong, collaborative relationships. This approach enhances operational efficiency and creates a reputable and sustainable brand.

4. Inventory Management Techniques

Effective inventory management is crucial for the success and sustainability of a fashion brand. It involves maintaining the right stock balance to meet customer demand without incurring excess costs. Proper inventory management ensures that your products are available when needed, reduces the risk of stockouts or overstock, and ultimately enhances operational efficiency and profitability.

Key Inventory Management Techniques

1. **Just-In-Time (JIT) Inventory**
    - JIT is a strategy where materials and products are ordered and received only as they are needed in the production process rather than being stored in inventory.
    - **Benefits**: Reduces holding costs, minimises waste, and ensures fresher inventory.
    - Zara is renowned for its JIT inventory system, which allows it to respond quickly to changing fashion trends and customer demands. By aligning production with real-time demand, Zara reduces excess inventory and ensures its stores are stocked with the latest fashions.

2. **Economic Order Quantity (EOQ)**

    - EOQ is a formula that determines the optimal order quantity that minimises the total inventory cost, including ordering and holding costs.
    - **Formula**: EOQ = $\sqrt{((2DS)/H)}$, where D is demand, S is ordering cost, and H is holding cost.
    - **Benefits**: Balances ordering and holding inventory costs, optimising stock levels.

3. **ABC Analysis**

    - ABC analysis categorises inventory into three groups—A, B, and C—based on their value and importance. 'A' items are the most valuable, 'B' items are of moderate value, and 'C' items are the least useful.
    - **Benefits**: Helps prioritise inventory management efforts, ensuring the most critical items receive attention.

Balancing Inventory Levels

- **Demand Forecasting**

    - Predicting future customer demand using historical data, market trends, and analytics.
    - **Benefits**: Helps maintain optimal inventory levels, reducing the risk of overstocking or stockouts.
    - Stitch Fix uses sophisticated data analytics to forecast demand and stock the right products in the right quantities.

- **Safety Stock**

    - Extra inventory is kept to prevent stockouts during demand fluctuations or supply chain disruptions.
    - **Formula**: Safety Stock = (Maximum Daily Usage x Maximum Lead Time) - (Average Daily Usage x Average Lead Time).

- **Benefits**: Provides a buffer against uncertainty in demand and supply.
- A fashion retailer calculates safety stock levels to ensure a buffer during peak seasons, such as the holiday shopping period.

Sustainable Inventory Practices

1. **Eco-Friendly Materials**

    - Source materials that are sustainable and have a lower environmental impact.
    - **Benefits**: Enhances brand reputation and meets consumer demand for sustainable products.
    - Everlane uses organic cotton and recycled materials, appealing to eco-conscious consumers.

2. **Waste Reduction**

    - Implement practices that minimise waste, such as recycling and upcycling.
    - **Benefits**: Reduces environmental impact and production costs.
    - Patagonia's Worn Wear programme encourages customers to recycle their old Patagonia products, reducing waste and promoting sustainability.

Effective inventory management combines strategic planning, advanced technology, and sustainability. By leveraging techniques like JIT, EOQ, and ABC analysis, and integrating technology such as IMS and RFID, fashion brands can optimise their inventory, reduce costs, and enhance customer satisfaction. This comprehensive approach ensures that your brand can meet market demands efficiently while maintaining a commitment to sustainability.

5. Technology in Inventory Management

In the fashion industry, managing inventory effectively ensures that products are available to meet customer demand while minimising excess stock and associated costs. Advanced technology has revolutionised inventory management, enabling fashion brands to track, manage, and optimise their inventory more accurately and efficiently. This section explores the various technologies transforming inventory management and their impact on operational efficiency and profitability.

Inventory Management Systems (IMS)

Inventory Management Systems (IMS) are software solutions that manage and track inventory levels, orders, sales, and deliveries in real-time.

Benefits

- **Accuracy and Efficiency**: IMS provides real-time visibility into inventory levels, reducing errors and manual tracking.
- **Automation**: Automates routine tasks such as reordering and inventory counts, freeing time for strategic activities.
- **Integration**: It integrates with other business systems, such as ERP (Enterprise Resource Planning) and POS (Point of Sale), for seamless operations.
- **ASOS**: ASOS utilises an advanced IMS to monitor inventory across its global distribution centres. This system enables real-time inventory tracking, reducing the risk of stockouts and overstock. The integration with their e-commerce platform ensures that inventory levels are updated instantly as orders are placed, enhancing customer satisfaction with accurate stock availability information.

Radio-Frequency Identification (RFID)

RFID technology uses electromagnetic fields to identify and track tags attached to inventory items automatically.

Benefits

- **Real-Time Tracking**: Provides real-time data on inventory levels, locations, and movements.
- **Labour Savings**: Reduces the need for manual counting and scanning, saving labour costs.
- **Enhanced Accuracy**: Increases inventory accuracy by reducing human error.
- **Levi's**: Levi's employs RFID technology in its stores to streamline inventory management. RFID tags are attached to each item, enabling the brand to track inventory in real-time, reduce shrinkage, and improve stock accuracy. This technology also enhances the customer experience by ensuring that the products they want are available when they visit the store.

Benefits of RFID Technology, Data Analytics, and AI

Definition: Data analytics involves analysing large datasets to uncover patterns, trends, and insights. Artificial Intelligence (AI) uses machine learning algorithms to predict future trends and automate decision-making processes.

Benefits

- **Demand Forecasting**: Predict future customer demand using historical data and trends, ensuring optimal inventory levels.
- **Personalised Recommendations**: Tailor product recommendations based on customer behaviour and preferences.

- **Inventory Optimisation**: Automate reordering processes and optimise stock levels to reduce holding costs and stockouts.

Example

- **Stitch Fix**: Stitch Fix uses AI and data analytics to personalise fashion recommendations for its customers. By analysing customer preferences, purchase history, and feedback, Stitch Fix can accurately predict which products to stock and in what quantities, optimising inventory management and reducing waste.

Cloud-Based Inventory Solutions

Cloud-based inventory management systems store data on remote servers, allowing access from anywhere with an internet connection.

Benefits

- **Scalability**: Easily scale up or down based on business needs without significant capital investment.
- **Accessibility**: Access inventory data in real-time from any location, enhancing flexibility and decision-making.
- **Cost-Effective**: Reduces the need for on-premises hardware and maintenance, lowering IT costs.
- **Glossier**: Glossier uses a cloud-based inventory management system to manage its global supply chain. This system provides real-time visibility into inventory levels across locations, enabling efficient stock management and quick responses to market changes.

Automation and Robotics

Automation and robotics involve using automated systems and robots to perform inventory management tasks such as picking, packing, and sorting.

Benefits

- **Increased Efficiency**: Robots can work faster and more accurately than humans, increasing throughput.
- **Cost Savings**: Reduces labour costs and minimises errors, leading to cost savings.
- **Scalability**: Easily scale operations up or down based on demand without the need for additional workforce.
- **Amazon**: Amazon's fulfilment centres use a combination of robotics and automation to manage inventory. Robots handle tasks such as moving inventory shelves to human workers, who pick and pack orders. This system enhances efficiency, reduces errors, and speeds up order fulfilment.

Technology in inventory management enables fashion brands to optimise their inventory processes, improve accuracy, reduce costs, and enhance customer satisfaction. By leveraging advanced systems such as IMS, RFID, AI, and automation, brands can stay competitive and responsive to market demands, ensuring long-term success.

6. Sustainability in Sourcing and Inventory Management

Sustainability and ethical sourcing have gained significant attention in today's business world. As the global population continues to grow, the demand for goods and services is also increasing rapidly, putting immense pressure on natural resources and the environment. Therefore, companies now focus on managing their inventories more efficiently to promote sustainability and ethical sourcing.

Inventory management controls the movement and storage of goods from the point of origin to the point of consumption. Effective inventory management ensures that the right products are available at the right time and helps reduce waste, improve efficiency, and lower costs.

Sustainability

Sustainability refers to the ability to maintain a certain level of production or consumption without depleting natural resources or causing harm to the environment. Inventory management plays a vital role in promoting sustainability in the following ways:

Reducing waste

Effective inventory management can reduce waste by always maintaining the correct inventory amount. This prevents overproduction, often leading to excess inventory that eventually becomes obsolete and ends up in landfills.

Lowering Energy Consumption

Inventory management can also help lower energy consumption by reducing the need for storage and transportation. By keeping inventory levels low and optimising delivery routes, businesses can minimise the energy required to store and transport goods.

Encouraging sustainable production

By optimising inventory levels, businesses can ensure that production is aligned with demand, reducing the need for excessive production. This, in turn, encourages sustainable production practices, as companies can focus on producing what is needed rather than producing excess goods that may go to waste.

Ethical Sourcing

Ethical sourcing refers to ensuring that products are obtained from suppliers who adhere to specific ethical standards, such as fair labour practices, environmental sustainability, and animal welfare. Inventory management plays a vital role in promoting ethical sourcing in the following ways:

Ensuring transparency

Effective inventory management can help ensure transparency in the supply chain by providing real-time data on inventory levels and supplier performance. This enables businesses to identify potential ethical issues in the supply chain and take corrective action.

Promoting responsible sourcing

Businesses can promote responsible sourcing practices by optimising inventory levels and ensuring transparency in the supply chain. This means companies can source products from suppliers that adhere to ethical standards, such as fair labour practices and environmental sustainability.

Encouraging Supplier Collaboration

Effective inventory management can also encourage supplier collaboration by providing suppliers with real-time data on inventory levels and demand. This enables suppliers to plan their production and delivery schedules better, reducing the risk of overproduction and waste.

An increasing environmental awareness, especially among some younger people, has begun a shift away from fast-fashion towards more ethical, sustainable, and environmentally friendly fashion.

Young and middle-aged men are most likely to stick solely to sustainable clothing brands, and those who do are more likely to buy second-hand or recycled clothes.

- Men between 25 and 44 are likely to say they only buy sustainable fashion.
- 73% of British consumers who only buy sustainable brands are also happy to buy second-hand clothes.
- 75% of Gen Z respondents said they bought pre-owned clothes to reduce consumption.

Despite generally having less disposable income, millennials are more likely to be willing to spend more on sustainable, environmentally conscious upcycled clothing and ethical fashion brands.

Do consumers want more sustainable fashion?

These seven market research statistics show substantial consumer demand for sustainable fashion.[43]

However, some consumers are worried about greenwashing in this space, and others don't know where to find sustainable clothing.

- 72% of US consumers are aware of sustainability and environmental issues surrounding the fashion industry.[44]
- 55% of US consumers are interested in buying sustainable clothing.
- However, 48% do not know where to find sustainable clothing brands.
- 69% of Vogue readers consider sustainability necessary when deciding on a new fashion purchase.

---

43 sustainable fashion statistics by
Arabella Ruiz
Category: Statistics
Updated: 18 March 2024
https://theroundup.org/sustainable-fashion-statistics/?utm_source=chatgpt.com

44 from a survey conducted by **Genomatica** and reported by **GlobeNewswire** on 26 May 2021

- 38% of consumers say that one of their main priorities is for fashion brands to reduce their environmental impact.
- 38% of Vogue readers buy as much sustainable fashion as possible, and 46% say they sometimes buy it. Only 2% are not interested in making sustainable purchases.
- ⅓ of US consumers would buy all their clothing at a sustainable store if they knew where to find one.

It's no secret that serious environmental concerns exist around the fashion industry's operations.

But how bad is it, and what might happen if the sustainable fashion revolution does not take off? These statistics lay bare the truth, some worse than expected.

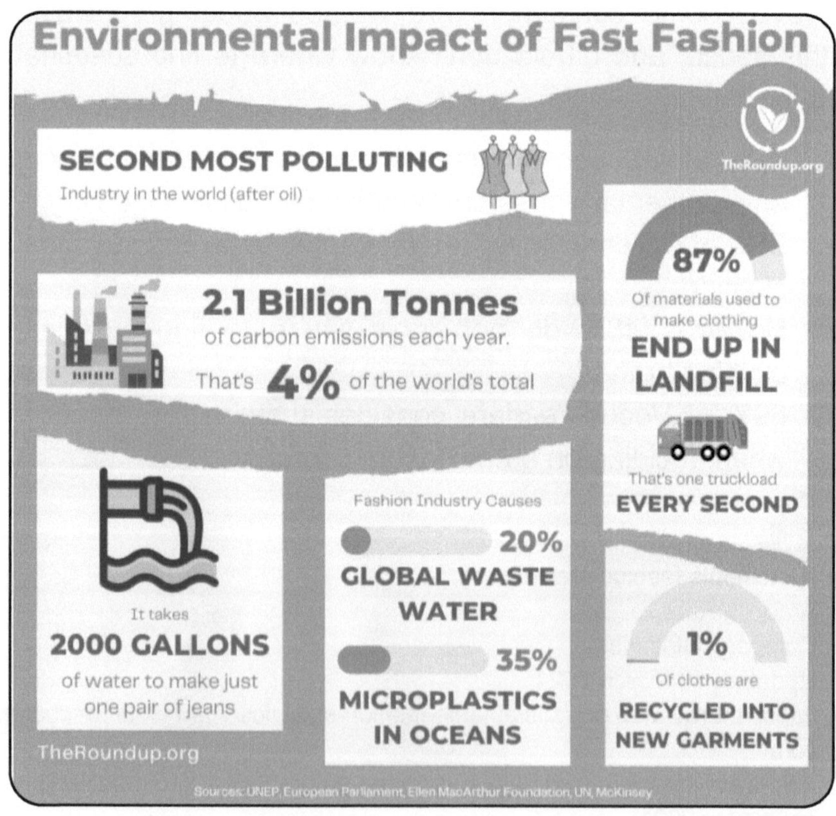

These statistics show how much the fashion industry contributes to water pollution and climate change.

- Fashion is considered to be the second-highest polluting industry in the world.
- The fashion industry produces 2.1 billion tonnes of carbon emissions annually, or around 4% of total global greenhouse gas emissions—more than shipping and aviation combined.
- Around 70% of the fashion industry's emissions came from upstream activities (these include the production of materials, preparation, and processing).
- 20% of global freshwater pollution is caused by textile treatment and dyeing.
- Switching to renewable, clean energy sources could reduce the clothing industry's carbon footprint by 63%.
- If no further action is taken over the next decade, the industry's GHG emissions will rise to around 2.7 billion tonnes annually by 2030, reflecting an annual volume growth rate of 2.7%.
- At its current rate, the fashion industry will use up 26% of the entire global carbon budget (based on a 2-degree scenario) by 2050.
- Making fashion a circular economy could reduce 33% of the CO2 emissions associated with textile production.

How much waste is due to fast-fashion?

- The statistics demonstrate that fast-fashion encourages overproduction, overbuying, and massive textile waste.
- Between 80 and 100 billion new clothing garments are produced every year.
- Global clothing production in 2000 was double what it was in 2014.
- 87% of the materials and fibres used to make clothing will end up in either incinerators or landfills.

- That's one truckload every second.
- Only 1% of clothes will get recycled into new garments.
- In the average UK household, ⅓ of clothes have not been worn in the last year.

Why is fast-fashion unsustainable?

Profits drive the fast-fashion industry, mainly using unsustainable materials in its products. Instead, these companies create garments using non-renewable resources, which are not sustainable by their very definition.

They also exploit workers in their supply chain who are subjected to unacceptable working conditions and do not receive a fair wage.

- The textile industry uses 98 million tonnes of non-renewable resources every year.
- 60% of all clothing materials are derived from plastic, which is made from fossil fuels. These include nylon, acrylic, and polyester.
- 93% of fashion companies still do not pay their workers a living wage.

How does fast-fashion affect water pollution?

The data show that the fashion sector does not use sustainable practices and significantly damages our rivers and oceans.

- Textile production uses 93 billion cubic metres of water every year.
- The fashion industry is responsible for 20% of total wastewater globally.
- Textile dyeing is the second-largest polluter of water globally, behind only oil.
- It takes 2,000 gallons of water to make just one pair of jeans.
- Synthetic man-made fibres account for 35% of microplastics released into our oceans.

Conclusion

It's no secret that the fashion industry is under intense public pressure due to the negative environmental impact of its carbon emissions, water consumption, and pollution.

But is that fair, and is sustainable fashion the answer?

These sustainable fashion statistics allow you to conclude based on evidence rather than opinion.

Are you concerned about the environmental and health impacts of synthetic fibres? Would you pay more for clothing made from sustainable raw materials such as organic cotton? Would you buy garments made from recycled plastic or fibres or shop second-hand?

The data show that the answer is yes for increasing consumers.

Key Takeaways from The Art of Sourcing and Inventory Management:

1. **Sourcing as a Strategic Pillar**
    - Effective sourcing is not just operational; it builds brand identity, sustainability, and market differentiation.
    - Brands like Patagonia excel by aligning sourcing practices with their environmental and social commitments.

2. **The Critical Role of Speed and Adaptability**
    - Agility in sourcing and inventory management is essential to address rapidly shifting consumer preferences, shorter trend cycles, and global competition.
    - Fast-fashion leaders like Zara demonstrate the advantage of agile supply chains in maintaining trend relevance and minimising unsold stock.

3. **Agile Design and Supply Chain Streamlining**
    - Implementing agile methodologies reduces product development cycles and enhances responsiveness to consumer feedback.
    - Technologies like ERP systems, local sourcing, and lean manufacturing streamline supply chains, reducing delays and improving cost efficiency.
4. **Technological Integration in Inventory Management**
    - AI, blockchain, IoT, and AR are transforming inventory practices by enhancing accuracy, reducing waste, and providing transparency.
    - Tools such as 3D modelling and IMS systems optimise inventory processes, improving production efficiency and customer satisfaction.
5. **Inventory Management Techniques for Efficiency and Sustainability**
    - Strategies like Just-In-Time (JIT), Economic Order Quantity (EOQ), and ABC Analysis balance stock levels to minimise costs and waste.
    - Sustainable practices, such as upcycling and eco-friendly materials, strengthen brand reputation and align with growing consumer demand for ethical products.
6. **Supplier Selection and Relationship Management**
    - Criteria for selecting suppliers include quality, cost, reliability, and sustainability.
    - Building strong relationships through communication, collaboration, and trust drives innovation and competitive advantage.

7. **Sustainability in Sourcing and Inventory**
   - Sustainable sourcing practices and waste reduction are no longer optional but necessary to align with consumer expectations and regulatory demands.
   - Programmes like Patagonia's Worn Wear illustrate how sustainability can reduce costs while fostering customer loyalty.
8. **Data-Driven Decision Making**
   - Real-time data integration through AI and predictive analytics enhances demand forecasting, reduces excess stock, and aligns production with actual demand.
   - Companies like Myntra and Nike use data analytics to refine inventory management and improve operational responsiveness.

Sourcing and inventory management are no longer back-office operations but strategic drivers of brand success in a competitive and fast-changing fashion industry. Prioritising agility, sustainability, and technology ensures brands remain relevant, efficient, and profitable.

Radio-Frequency Identification (RFID)

- **Real-Time Tracking:** Provides real-time data on inventory levels, locations, and movements.
- **Labour Savings:** Reduces the need for manual counting and scanning, saving labour costs.
- **Enhanced Accuracy:** Increases inventory accuracy by reducing human error.

Data Analytics and Artificial Intelligence (AI)

- **Demand Forecasting:** Predicts future customer demand using historical data and trends.

- **Personalised Recommendations:** Tailor's product recommendations are based on customer behaviour and preferences.
- **Inventory Optimisation:** Automates reordering processes and optimises stock levels to reduce holding costs and stockouts.

Cloud-Based Inventory Solutions

- **Scalability:** Easily scale up or down based on business needs.
- **Accessibility:** Access inventory data in real-time from any location.
- **Cost-Effective:** Reduces the need for on-premises hardware and maintenance, lowering IT costs.

Automation and Robotics

- **Increased Efficiency:** Robots can work faster and more accurately than humans.
- **Cost Savings:** Reduces labour costs and minimises errors.
- **Scalability:** Easily scale operations up or down based on demand.

Advanced technology such as RFID, data analytics, AI, cloud-based solutions, and automation can significantly optimise inventory management. These innovations improve accuracy, reduce costs, and enhance customer satisfaction, allowing fashion brands to stay competitive and responsive to market demands.

Sustainability in Sourcing and Inventory Management

Growing Importance: The increasing demand for goods puts pressure on natural resources, emphasising the need for sustainability and ethical sourcing.

Efficient Inventory Management: Ensures the right products are available at the right time, reducing waste, improving efficiency, and lowering costs.

Promoting Sustainability

Reducing Waste: Effective inventory management prevents overproduction and reduces obsolete excess inventory.

Lowering Energy Consumption: Energy consumption is reduced by minimising storage and transportation needs.

Encouraging Sustainable Production: Optimised inventory levels ensure production is aligned with demand, promoting sustainable practices.

Ethical Sourcing

Transparency: Real-time data on inventory levels and supplier performance ensure transparency in the supply chain.

Responsible Sourcing: Businesses can source products from suppliers adhering to ethical standards, such as fair labour practices and environmental sustainability.

Supplier Collaboration: Real-time data allows suppliers to plan production and delivery schedules better, reducing overproduction and waste.

Consumer Trends Towards Sustainability

Shifting Preferences: Increasing environmental awareness, especially among younger people, is shifting demand towards ethical and sustainable fashion.

Demand for Sustainable Fashion: Consumers are increasingly interested in buying sustainable clothing, but some face challenges in finding sustainable brands.

Environmental Impact of the Fashion Industry

Carbon Emissions: The fashion industry contributes significantly to global greenhouse gas emissions and water pollution.

Fast-Fashion Waste: Fast-fashion encourages overproduction, leading to massive textile waste.

Unsustainable Practices: Non-renewable resources and poor working conditions in the fast-fashion industry make it unsustainable.

Public Pressure: The fashion industry faces intense public pressure due to its environmental impact.

Consumer Willingness: Many consumers are willing to pay more for sustainable and ethically produced clothing.

Sustainable Fashion Movement: The data indicates a growing movement towards sustainable fashion, driven by consumer awareness and demand.

By focusing on sustainability and ethical sourcing, businesses can meet consumer demand, reduce environmental impact, and ensure long-term success.

Chapter 10

Scaling Your Brand

"Scaling with Soul"

> *"Don't look at small business as a means to an end and a way to make money until the corporation hires you; look at it as a chance to create something of immeasurable value and beauty in a world that desperately needs it."*
> *– Michael Gerber.*

Scaling a fashion brand is not merely a matter of increasing production or expanding your product line; it is a strategic endeavour encompassing growth and sustainability. Achieving successful scaling involves enhancing operational efficiency, expanding market reach, diversifying product offerings, and leveraging the latest technology. This chapter will explore these aspects in detail, providing actionable insights and real-world examples to guide you through scaling your fashion brand effectively.

Expanding into new markets is a critical step in scaling your brand. This can involve geographic expansion, tapping into new demographic segments, or increasing online presence. Effective market expansion strategies are rooted in thorough market research and a deep understanding of local consumer behaviour.

H&M's expansion into emerging markets like India and China demonstrates the importance of understanding local cultures and consumer preferences.

Offering a diverse range of products can help mitigate risks and cater to a broader customer base. Product diversification can involve introducing new categories, collaborating with other brands, or launching limited editions.

Nike's diversification from footwear to apparel, accessories and sports equipment has significantly contributed to its market dominance.

Supreme's limited-edition collaborations with brands like Louis Vuitton create buzz and drive sales.

Technology is a powerful enabler of scalability. From advanced data analytics to personalised marketing and efficient inventory management, leveraging technology can enhance every aspect of your business operations.

ASOS uses AI to personalise customer experiences and optimise logistics.

Scaling a fashion brand is a multifaceted process that requires careful planning, strategic execution, and continuous adaptation. By focusing on operational efficiency, market expansion, product diversification, and leveraging technology, you can build a robust framework for growth and sustainability. This chapter will provide the tools, examples, and insights needed to scale your brand successfully, drawing from real-world case studies, statistical data, and actionable strategies.

Let's dive into these essential components and explore how to take your fashion brand to new heights.

Assessing Readiness for Scaling

Before scaling your fashion brand, it is crucial to assess your readiness thoroughly. Scaling without proper preparation can lead to operational inefficiencies, financial strain, and a potential decline in product quality or customer satisfaction. This section will provide a detailed exploration of the key factors to consider when assessing your readiness for scaling.

Operational Readiness: Operational efficiency forms the backbone of a scalable fashion brand. As your business grows, so do the demands on your supply chain, production processes, and inventory management. Operational efficiency ensures you can meet these demands without compromising quality or incurring excessive costs. This section will explore strategies such as automation, improved logistics, and sustainable practices.

Production Capacity

- Evaluate whether your current production processes can handle increased demand. Can your suppliers and manufacturers scale alongside you? If not, consider investing in new technology or forming additional partnerships.
- **Example**: Zara's success in the fast-fashion industry is mainly due to its highly responsive supply chain that can adapt quickly to changes in demand and fashion trends.

Supply Chain Robustness

- Assess the strength and reliability of your supply chain. Any weaknesses here can cause significant disruptions as you scale.

Quality Control

- Ensure that increasing production does not compromise your product quality. Implementing robust quality control measures is essential.
- Lululemon maintains high product quality standards even as it scales, which has helped the brand build a loyal customer base.

Financial Readiness

1. **Cash Flow Management**
   - A healthy cash flow is critical for scaling. You need sufficient capital to invest in inventory, marketing, staffing, and other operational costs.
   - The Small Business Administration reports that 82% of businesses fail due to cash flow problems. Proper financial planning can mitigate this risk.
2. **Funding Options**
   - Explore various funding options such as reinvesting profits, securing loans, or attracting venture capital. Each option has its benefits and risks.
   - Warby Parker used a combination of venture capital funding and strategic reinvestment of profits to scale its operations successfully.

Market Readiness

1. **Market Demand**
   - Conduct thorough market research to ensure sufficient demand for your expanded product offerings. Identify new target segments and understand their needs.

  - According to a Nielsen survey, 59% of consumers prefer to buy new products from familiar brands[45], highlighting the importance of brand loyalty in scaling.

2. **Competitive Landscape**
  - Analyse your competition to identify opportunities and threats. Understanding your competitors' strengths and weaknesses can help you position your brand more effectively.
  - H&M's expansion into emerging markets was based on detailed market research and competitive analysis, allowing the brand to tailor its offerings to local consumer preferences.

Technology Readiness

- **Digital Infrastructure**
  - Investing in robust digital infrastructure is essential for managing increased traffic and transactions as you scale. This includes upgrading your website, implementing CRM systems, and using analytics tools.
  - ASOS uses advanced AI and machine learning algorithms to personalise customer experiences and manage logistics efficiently.
- **Automation**
  - Automating repetitive tasks can free up resources and improve efficiency. Consider automation for areas

---

45 https://rbr.com/consumers-more-likely-to-buy-new-items-from-familiar-brands/
Consumers more likely to buy new items from familiar brands
By cmarcucci - January 22, 2013

like inventory management, customer service, and marketing.

- A Deloitte study found that automation can reduce operational costs by up to 30% while increasing efficiency and accuracy.

Readiness Factor	Key Considerations	Example/Statistic
Production Capacity	Ability to meet increased demand	Zara's responsive supply chain
Cash Flow Management	Sufficient capital for scaling	82% of businesses fail due to cash flow issues (SBA)
Market Demand	Sufficient demand for new products	59% of consumers prefer familiar brands (Nielsen)
Digital Infrastructure	Robust systems to manage increased traffic	ASOS's use of AI and machine learning

Assessing readiness for scaling involves a comprehensive evaluation of your operational, financial, market, and technological capabilities. By meticulously planning and addressing potential challenges, you can ensure a smooth and successful scaling process for your fashion brand. This assessment will provide the foundation for making informed decisions and strategically positioning your brand for sustained growth.

Expanding Market Reach

Expanding your market reach in the competitive fashion world is essential for scaling your brand and achieving long-term success. This involves extending your presence to new geographic locations, tapping into diverse demographic segments, and leveraging digital platforms to broaden your audience. Effective market expansion strategies increase your customer base and enhance your brand's visibility and profitability.

Geographic Expansion

Geographic expansion allows you to access new markets and reach a broader audience. It can involve entering new regions within your current country or expanding internationally. Each market has unique opportunities and challenges, so thorough research and strategic planning is crucial.

1. **Domestic Expansion**: Warby Parker, initially an online-only brand, gradually expanded its presence with physical stores across the United States. This move helped them reach customers who prefer in-person shopping experiences. Wrogn in India started only with Myntra online. After seeing great success in online stores, the Brand is expanding into offline stores.
   - **Strategy**: Identify underserved regions and tailor your marketing strategies to local preferences and needs.
2. **International Expansion**
   - H&M's expansion into markets like India and China. By understanding local cultures and consumer behaviours, H&M successfully adapted its product offerings and marketing strategies to resonate with new audiences.
   - **Statistics**: According to Statista, global fashion retail sales are expected to reach $2.25 trillion by 2025, highlighting the potential for international market growth.

Demographic Segmentation

Tapping into new demographic segments can help diversify your customer base and drive growth. This involves understanding different consumer groups' specific needs, preferences, and behaviours and tailoring your offerings accordingly.

1. **Age Groups**
    - Levi's expanded its product lines to appeal to younger and older demographics. Levi's broadened its market reach by offering trendy designs for millennials and classic styles for older consumers.
2. **Lifestyle Segments**
    - Nike's segmentation strategy targets athletes, casual wearers, and fashion-conscious consumers. This has allowed Nike to cater to various needs and preferences, driving overall brand growth.

Digital Expansion

Leveraging digital platforms is critical for reaching a global audience and enhancing brand visibility. Digital expansion strategies can significantly boost online sales and brand engagement.

1. **E-commerce Platforms**
    - ASOS, a digital-first fashion brand, has successfully leveraged its online platform to reach customers worldwide. Its user-friendly website, mobile app, and efficient logistics have contributed to its rapid growth.
2. **Social Media Marketing**
    - **Example**: Fashion Nova uses Instagram to engage customers and promote its products. Fashion Nova has built a large and loyal following by partnering with influencers and creating visually appealing content.
    - According to a Sprout Social report, 77% of consumers are more likely to buy from brands they follow on social media.[46]

46 from a report by **Sprout Social** titled **"The Future of Social Media: New Data for 2021 & Beyond."**

3. **SEO and SEM**
    - **Strategy**: Implement search engine optimisation (SEO) and search engine marketing (SEM) strategies to improve your online visibility and attract more customers to your website.

- **Zara**: Zara's global expansion strategy involves a mix of physical stores and an online presence. The company's ability to adapt quickly to local markets and trends has been key to its success.
- **Everlane**: Everlane's focus on transparency and ethical practices has resonated with a global audience, helping it significantly expand its market reach.

Key Metrics to Track

- **Market Share**: Monitor changes in your market share as you expand into new regions and segments.
- **Customer Acquisition Cost (CAC)**: Track the cost of acquiring new customers to ensure your expansion strategies are cost-effective.
- **Return on Investment (ROI)**: Measure the ROI of your marketing campaigns and expansion initiatives to evaluate their effectiveness.

Expanding market reach is a multifaceted process that involves geographic expansion, demographic segmentation, and leveraging digital platforms. You can effectively scale your fashion brand and achieve sustainable growth by strategically targeting new markets and utilising data-driven insights.

Product Line Expansion

Expanding your product line is a strategic approach to scaling your fashion brand. It involves introducing new products or categories that complement your existing offerings, catering to diverse customer needs and preferences. This increases your brand's market reach and helps mitigate risks by reducing dependency on a single product line. Effective product line expansion can drive revenue growth, enhance customer loyalty, and reinforce your brand's position in the competitive fashion industry.

Understanding Product Line Expansion

Product line expansion is more than adding new items to your inventory. It requires a deep understanding of your market, customer preferences, and overall brand vision. The key is ensuring new products align with your brand identity and resonate with your target audience.

Steps to Successful Product Line Expansion

1. **Market Research and Consumer Insights**

    - Conduct thorough market research to identify market gaps and understand customer needs. Gather insights through surveys, focus groups, and data analytics.

    For example, Nike uses consumer insights to identify new opportunities for product development. The company introduced its yoga apparel line in response to the growing demand for wellness and fitness products.

2. **Competitive Analysis**

    - Analyse your competitors' product lines to identify opportunities and threats. Understand what works for them and where they fall short.
    - Zara's ability to adapt quickly to fashion trends and introduce new products has helped it stay ahead of the competition in the fast-fashion industry.

3. **Product Development**
   - Develop new products that complement your existing offerings. This could involve new styles, colours, or even entirely new categories.
   - Levi's expanded from jeans to a wide range of apparel and accessories, broadening its market appeal.
4. **Testing and Feedback**
   - Before a full-scale launch, test new products with a small segment of your audience. Gather feedback and make necessary adjustments.

Key Considerations for Product Line Expansion

1. **Brand Alignment**
   - Ensure that new products align with your brand's identity and values. This consistency helps maintain brand integrity and customer trust.
2. **Customer Experience**
   - Focus on enhancing the customer experience with the new products. This includes quality, design, and usability.
   - **Example**: Apple's expansion into wearables with the Apple Watch maintained the brand's commitment to innovation and user experience. Decathlon's product expansion revolves around sports.
3. **Supply Chain Management**
   - Evaluate and optimise your supply chain to handle the increased complexity of product line expansion. Efficient logistics and inventory management are crucial for timely delivery and customer satisfaction.

By carefully planning and executing product line expansion, you can unlock new growth opportunities for your fashion brand. This strategic move boosts revenue and strengthens your brand's market position, making it more resilient and adaptable to changing market dynamics.

Enhancing Operational Efficiency

Operational efficiency is critical to scaling your fashion brand successfully. As your business grows, so do the complexities of managing production, supply chains, inventory, and customer service. Enhancing operational efficiency means optimising these processes to reduce costs, improve quality, and increase speed to market. This section will explore strategies and tools for achieving operational excellence, supported by specific examples, statistics, and insights.

Key Strategies for Enhancing Operational Efficiency

Automation and Technology Integration:

Lean Manufacturing and Just-in-Time (JIT) Production:

Supply Chain Optimisation:

Quality Control and Continuous Improvement:

Sustainable Practices:

Operational Efficiency Metrics

Metric	Before Improvement	After Improvement	Efficiency Gain
Inventory Turnover	4 times/year	6 times/year	50%
Lead Time (Production)	30 days	20 days	33%
Production Cost per Unit	$15	$12	20%
Defect Rate	5%	2%	60%

Enhancing operational efficiency is not a one-time effort but an ongoing process that requires continuous monitoring and improvement. You can build a robust operational framework that supports your brand's growth and scalability by leveraging automation, adopting lean practices, optimising the supply chain, maintaining strict quality control, and integrating sustainable practices.

6. Leveraging Data and Analytics

In a dynamic and competitive world, data and analytics are powerful tools to transform your brand's growth trajectory. Leveraging data effectively can provide deep insights into consumer behaviour, market trends, and operational efficiency, enabling you to make informed decisions and drive strategic initiatives. This section will delve into how fashion brands can harness the power of data and analytics to scale effectively, supported by specific examples, statistics, charts, and survey results.

Data and analytics are essential for understanding customers, optimising operations, and driving growth. Collecting and analysing data can help you gain valuable insights into market trends, tailor product offerings, and enhance the overall customer experience.

Key Areas to Leverage Data and Analytics

1. **Customer Insights and Personalisation**

   Customer Segmentation: Use data to segment your customers based on demographics, buying behaviour, and preferences. This allows you to tailor your marketing strategies to specific segments, improving engagement and conversion rates.

   Personalised Marketing: Data-driven personalisation enhances the customer experience by delivering relevant content, offers, and product recommendations.

ASOS uses data analytics to personalise product recommendations and marketing emails, increasing customer satisfaction and sales.

2. **Demand Forecasting and Inventory Management**

   Predictive Analytics: Use predictive analytics to forecast demand and optimise inventory levels. This will help reduce stockouts and overstock situations.

   Zara leverages data analytics for real-time inventory management, ensuring it has the right products in the right quantities at the right time.

3. **Marketing and Sales Optimisation**

   Customer Journey Analysis: Analyse data to understand the customer journey and identify touchpoints influencing purchasing decisions. This helps optimise marketing strategies and improve ROI.

   Nike uses data analytics to track customer interactions across multiple channels, allowing it to optimise its marketing efforts and improve customer engagement.

   Performance Metrics: Monitor key performance indicators (KPIs) such as conversion rates, customer acquisition costs (CAC), and lifetime value (LTV) to evaluate the effectiveness of your marketing campaigns.

4. **Product Development and Innovation**

   Trend Analysis: Use data to identify emerging trends and consumer preferences, informing product development and innovation.

   Stitch Fix uses data analytics to identify fashion trends and customise its clothing offerings, resulting in a highly personalised shopping experience.

5. **Operational Efficiency and Cost Reduction**

   Process Optimisation: Analyse operational data to identify inefficiencies and optimise processes. This can include improving production workflows, reducing waste, and enhancing supply chain management.

Impact of Data-Driven Strategies on Key Metrics

Metric	Before Analytics	After Analytics	Improvement (%)
Customer Acquisition Cost (CAC)	$50	$40	20%
Inventory Turnover Rate	4 times/year	6 times/year	50%
Conversion Rate	2.5%	3.5%	40%
Lead Time (Production)	30 days	20 days	33%

- **Netflix**: While not a fashion brand, Netflix's use of data analytics to personalise content recommendations provides a compelling example of how data can drive customer engagement and retention. Similarly, fashion brands can use data to personalise product recommendations and marketing messages.
- **Amazon**: Amazon's use of predictive analytics for inventory management and demand forecasting has set operational efficiency benchmarks. Fashion brands can adopt similar strategies to optimise their supply chains and reduce costs.

Leveraging data and analytics is essential for scaling your fashion brand effectively. By harnessing the power of data, you can gain valuable insights, optimise your operations, and drive growth. This section provides a comprehensive overview of the key areas where data and analytics can significantly impact, supported by real-world examples, statistics, and visual aids.

Building a Strong Brand Community

In the competitive fashion world, creating a strong brand community is not just a strategy but a necessity for long-term success. A dedicated brand community fosters customer loyalty, encourages word-of-mouth marketing, and provides valuable insights to help shape your brand's growth. Building a community around your brand involves creating meaningful connections with your customers, engaging them in authentic conversations, and making them feel valued and part of your brand's journey.

The Importance of a Brand Community

A robust brand community is an extension of your brand, where loyal customers become brand advocates. These advocates not only support your brand but also help attract new customers through their genuine endorsements. According to a study by Nielsen, 92% of consumers trust recommendations from friends and family over any other form of advertising, highlighting the impact of a strong community.

Key Strategies for Building a Brand Community

1. **Engaging Content and Storytelling**
    - **Authentic Storytelling**: Share your brand's story, values, and mission through engaging content. Authentic storytelling helps build an emotional connection with your audience.
    - **User-Generated Content**: Encourage customers to share their experiences with your brand. User-generated content (UGC) boosts engagement and serves as social proof.

2. **Social Media Engagement**
   - **Active Presence**: Maintain an active presence on social media platforms. Engage with your audience through comments, direct messages, and interactive content like polls and Q&A sessions.
   - **community Hashtags**: Create and promote unique hashtags to encourage community participation. Hashtags can help gather content, foster community spirit, and increase brand visibility.
3. **Exclusive Events and Experiences**
   - **Brand Events**: Host exclusive events, both online and offline, to bring your community together. Events provide an opportunity for direct interaction and create memorable experiences.
   - **Virtual Communities**: Create online communities or forums where customers can connect, share experiences, and engage with the brand. These platforms can be a hub for discussions, feedback, and brand updates.
4. **Loyalty Programmes and Rewards**
   - **Loyalty Programmes**: Implement loyalty programmes to reward repeat customers and encourage long-term engagement. Loyalty programmes can include points systems, exclusive discounts, and early access to new products.
   - **Gamification:** Incorporate gamification elements into your loyalty programmes to make them more engaging and fun for customers.

- Patagonia: Patagonia has built a strong community around its commitment to environmental activism. Patagonia has fostered a loyal and engaged community by involving customers in their sustainability efforts and sharing impactful stories.

- Warby Parker engages its community through social initiatives and transparent business practices. Its Buy a Pair, give a Pair programme resonates with socially conscious consumers and builds community.

Building a strong brand community involves more than just marketing; it's about creating a sense of belonging and connection among your customers. By leveraging engaging content, social media, exclusive events, loyalty programmes, and authentic storytelling, you can foster a dedicated community that supports your brand and drives its growth.

8. Measuring Success and Adjusting Strategies

As your fashion brand scales, continuously measuring success and adapting your strategies is crucial for sustained market growth and relevance. This process involves evaluating your performance through key metrics, understanding market trends, and being agile in strategic adjustments. Measuring success helps track progress and identify improvement areas, ensuring your brand remains competitive and aligned with its goals.

The Importance of Measuring Success

Measuring success provides a clear picture of your brand's performance in various aspects, such as sales, customer engagement, and operational efficiency. It enables you to make data-driven decisions, optimize resources, and enhance effectiveness. According to a study by Gartner, companies that utilise data-driven decision-making are 23 times more likely to acquire customers, six times as likely to retain customers, and 19 times as likely to be profitable.

Key Metrics to Track

1. **Revenue Growth**
2. **Customer Acquisition Cost (CAC)**
    - CAC = Total Marketing and sales Expenses / Number of New Customers Acquired.
    - For example, if you spent $50,000 on marketing and acquired 500 new customers, your CAC would be $100.

3. **Customer Lifetime Value (CLV)**
    - CLV estimates a customer's total revenue during their relationship with your brand.
    - CLV = (Average Purchase Value) x (Number of Purchases per Year) x (Average Customer Lifespan).
    - Example: If a customer spends $100 per purchase, makes four purchases per year, and stays with your brand for five years, their CLV is $2,000.
    - Survey Results: A study by Harvard Business Review found that increasing CLV by 5% can boost profits by 25-95%.

4. **Net Promoter Score (NPS)**
    - NPS measures customer loyalty and satisfaction by asking customers how likely they are to recommend your brand to others.
    - Scale: Customers rate on a scale of 0-10, with promoters (9-10), passives (7-8), and detractors (0-6).
    - Example: An NPS score of 50 is considered excellent, indicating high customer satisfaction and loyalty.
    - Statistics: According to Bain & Company, companies with high NPS grow faster and have higher customer retention rates.

Adjusting Strategies Based on Metrics

1. Identifying Trends and Insights

- Analyse Data: Regularly analyse the data collected from your key metrics to identify trends and insights. This will help you understand what is working and what needs improvement.
- Example: If your CAC is rising, investigate the effectiveness of your marketing channels and allocate resources to the most cost-effective ones.

2. Agility in Strategy Adjustments

- Be Proactive: Adjust your strategies based on the insights gained from your metrics. This includes tweaking marketing campaigns, optimising sales processes, and improving customer engagement tactics.

3. Implementing Continuous Improvement

- Feedback Loops: Establish feedback loops to gather customer insights and continuously improve your products and services. This will help maintain customer satisfaction and loyalty.

Measuring success and adjusting strategies are vital for your fashion brand's continuous growth and sustainability. By tracking key performance metrics, analysing data, and being agile, you can ensure your brand remains competitive and aligned with its long-term goals.

Key Takeaways from Scaling Your Brand

1. Strategic Scaling: Scaling involves more than increasing production; it also requires growth and sustainability. Key aspects include operational efficiency, market expansion, product diversification, and technology leverage.

2. Market Expansion: Expanding into new markets involves understanding local consumer behaviour and preferences.

3. Product Diversification: Offering diverse products can mitigate risks and cater to a broader customer base. New categories, brand collaborations, or limited editions can achieve this.

4. Leveraging Technology: Technology enhances scalability through data analytics, personalised marketing, and efficient inventory management.

5. Comprehensive Planning: Scaling requires careful planning, strategic execution, and continuous adaptation. Focus areas include:

- Operational Efficiency: Streamlining processes to improve productivity and reduce costs.
- Market Expansion: Identifying and entering new markets with effective strategies.
- Product Diversification: Broadening the product range to attract diverse customer segments.
- Technology Integration: Utilising advanced technologies to enhance business operations.

"Assessing Readiness for Scaling"

Operational Readiness

- **Efficiency in Operations:** Crucial for a scalable brand; includes automation, improved logistics, and sustainable practices.
- **Production Capacity:** Evaluate if current processes can handle increased demand; consider technology investments or new partnerships.
- **Supply Chain Robustness:** Assess strength and reliability to prevent disruptions.
- **Quality Control:** Maintain product quality with robust measures.

Financial Readiness

- **Cash Flow Management:** Essential for scaling; requires sufficient capital for inventory, marketing, staffing, etc.
- • **Funding Options:** Reinvesting profits, securing loans, or attracting venture capital.

Market Readiness

- **Market Demand:** Thorough research is needed to ensure sufficient demand for expanded offerings and identify new target segments.
- **Competitive Landscape:** Analyse competitors to identify opportunities and threats.

Technology Readiness

- **Digital Infrastructure:** Invest in robust infrastructure to increase traffic and transactions, upgrade websites, implement CRM systems, and use analytics.
- **Automation:** Reduces operational costs and improves efficiency.

Expanding Market Reach

1. **Geographic Expansion**
    - Expanding into new regions domestically and internationally is crucial for increasing market reach and brand visibility.
    - Key strategies involve thorough market research and tailoring marketing efforts to local preferences.

Domestic Expansion

- Expanding to underserved regions within your country helps target untapped markets and boost brand recognition.

International Expansion

- International markets offer significant growth potential, as global fashion retail sales are predicted to reach $2.25 trillion by 2025.

Demographic Segmentation

- Targeting specific demographic groups allows for a diverse customer base and market growth. This includes tailoring products for different age groups and lifestyle segments.

Digital Expansion

- Digital platforms, including e-commerce, social media, and SEO/SEM strategies, are vital in expanding market reach and enhancing brand visibility globally.

Key Metrics

- Monitoring important metrics like Market Share, Customer Acquisition Cost (CAC), and Return on Investment (ROI) helps assess the effectiveness and cost efficiency of expansion efforts.

Data-Driven Insights

- Using data and insights to inform decisions ensures your market expansion strategy is targeted, efficient, and aligned with consumer preferences. Fashion brands can scale and achieve sustainable growth by strategically expanding into new regions and segments,

Key Takeaways from "Product Line Expansion":

Understanding Product Line Expansion

- **Strategic Approach:** Expanding your product line involves introducing new products or categories that complement existing offerings and cater to diverse customer needs.
- **Market and Customer Insight** requires a deep understanding of market gaps, customer preferences, and the overall brand vision to ensure alignment with the brand identity.

Steps to Successful Product Line Expansion

- **Market Research and Consumer Insights:** Conduct thorough research to identify gaps and understand customer needs.
- **Competitive Analysis:** Analyse competitors to identify opportunities and threats.
- **Product Development:** Develop new products that complement existing offerings.
- **Testing and Feedback:** Before a full-scale launch, test new products with a small segment to gather feedback and adjust.

Key Considerations for Product Line Expansion

- **Brand Alignment:** Ensure new products align with the brand's identity and values.
- **Customer Experience:** Focus on enhancing the customer experience with quality, design, and usability.
- **Supply Chain Management:** Optimise the supply chain to handle the increased complexity of product line expansion.

Enhancing Operational Efficiency

Key Strategies for Enhancing Operational Efficiency

- **Automation and Technology Integration:** Utilise technology to streamline processes.
- **Lean Manufacturing and Just-in-Time (JIT) Production:** Adopt lean practices to reduce waste and improve efficiency.
- **Supply Chain Optimisation:** Enhance supply chain management to ensure timely delivery and customer satisfaction.
- **Quality Control and Continuous Improvement:** Maintain strict quality control and pursue continuous improvement.
- **Sustainable Practices:** Integrate sustainable practices into operations.

Leveraging Data and Analytics

Key Areas to Leverage Data and Analytics

- **Customer Insights and Personalisation:** Use data to segment customers and personalise marketing.
- **Demand Forecasting and Inventory Management:** Use predictive analytics to forecast demand and optimise inventory.
- **Marketing and sales Optimisation:** Analyse customer journey and monitor performance metrics.
- **Product Development and Innovation:** Use data to identify trends and inform product development.
- **Operational Efficiency and Cost Reduction:** Analyse operational data to optimise processes and reduce costs.

Expanding your product line and enhancing operational efficiency are crucial for scaling your fashion brand. Leveraging data and analytics provides valuable insights, optimises operations, and drives growth. By adopting these strategies, you can build a resilient and adaptable brand capable of meeting market demands and sustaining growth.

“Building a Strong Brand Community” and “Measuring Success and Adjusting Strategies”

Building a Strong Brand Community

- **Importance:** A dedicated brand community fosters loyalty, encourages word-of-mouth marketing, and provides valuable insights.

Key Strategies for Building a Brand Community

- **Engaging Content and Storytelling**
  - **Authentic Storytelling:** Share your brand’s story, values, and mission to build an emotional connection.
  - **User-Generated Content:** Encourage customers to share their experiences, boosting engagement and serving as social proof.
- **Social Media Engagement**
  - **Active Presence:** Engage with your audience through comments, direct messages, polls, and Q&A sessions.
  - **Community Hashtags:** Promote unique hashtags to encourage community participation and increase visibility.
- **Exclusive Events and Experiences**
  - **Brand Events:** Host exclusive online and offline events to unite your community.
  - **Virtual Communities:** Create online forums for customers to connect, share experiences, and engage with the brand.

- **Loyalty Programmes and Rewards**
    - **Loyalty Programmes:** Reward repeat customers and encourage long-term engagement through points systems, discounts, and early access.
    - **Gamification:** Incorporate gamification elements to make loyalty programmes more engaging and fun.

Measuring Success and Adjusting Strategies

Importance of Measuring Success

- **Data-Driven Decisions:** Provide a clear picture of brand performance and enable optimisation of resources.
    - Companies that use data-driven decision-making are 23 times more likely to acquire customers, six times more likely to retain customers, and 19 times more likely to be profitable.

Key Metrics to Track

- **Revenue Growth:** Measures overall financial performance.
- **Customer Acquisition Cost (CAC)**
    - **Formula:** CAC = Total Marketing and sales Expenses / Number of New Customers Acquired.
- **Customer Lifetime Value (CLV)**
    - **Formula:** CLV = (Average Purchase Value) x (Number of Purchases per Year) x (Average Customer Lifespan).
    - Increasing CLV by 5% can boost profits by 25-95%.
- **Net Promoter Score (NPS)**
    - **Scale:** Customers rate the likelihood of recommendation on a scale of 0-10.

 - Companies with a high NPS grow faster and have higher customer retention rates.

Adjusting Strategies Based on Metrics

- **Identifying Trends and Insights:** Analyse data to identify trends and insights.
- **Agility in Strategy Adjustments:** Based on insights, adjust strategies to improve marketing campaigns, sales processes, and customer engagement.

Implementing Continuous Improvement: Establish feedback loops for continuous product and service improvement.

Building a strong brand community and continuously measuring success is crucial for your fashion brand's long-term growth and sustainability. Engage customers through authentic storytelling, social media, and loyalty programmes using key metrics to track performance and adjust strategies for optimal results.

Chapter 11

Leading with Vision – Building a Strong Team and Culture

"Fashion Leadership Beyond the Office"

> *"Good business leaders create a vision, articulate the vision, passionately own the vision, and relentlessly drive it to completion." – Jack Welch.*

Fashion organisations need to adapt their employee strategies to meet the unique needs and preferences of new generation employees, such as Millennials and generation Z. Here are some keyways to do this:

New generation employees are digital natives who are comfortable with technology. Fashion organisations should integrate advanced digital tools and platforms for communication, collaboration, and project management. This includes using social media for marketing, e-commerce platforms, and digital design tools.

Millennials and Gen Z value continuous learning and career development. Providing opportunities for upskilling and reskilling, such as online courses, workshops, and mentorship programmes, can help keep them engaged and motivated.

New generation employees prefer a collaborative work environment where they can share ideas and work in teams.

Creating a culture that values diversity and inclusion and encourages open communication can help attract and retain these employees.

Work-life balance is a top priority for Millennials and Gen Z. Offering flexible work arrangements, such as remote work options and flexible hours, can help meet their needs and improve job satisfaction.

New generation employees seek meaningful work that aligns with their values and allows them to make a positive impact. To attract and retain these employees, fashion organisations should emphasise their commitment to sustainability, ethical practices, and social responsibility.

Regularly recognising and rewarding employees' contributions can boost morale and motivation. Implementing recognition programmes, performance-based incentives, and career advancement opportunities can help keep the new generation of employees engaged.

Prioritising employee well-being through wellness programmes, mental health support, and a healthy work environment can improve overall job satisfaction and productivity.

By adapting their employee strategies to meet the needs of new generation employees, fashion organisations can create a more engaged, motivated and loyal workforce.

In the fashion industry, leadership extends far beyond the office walls. Leading with vision involves building a strong team and fostering a culture that resonates with the brand's core values and mission. As the fashion landscape continues to evolve, the role of a leader becomes increasingly dynamic and multifaceted. The essential elements of effective leadership in the fashion industry, as well as emphasising the importance of cultivating a cohesive team and nurturing a positive organisational culture, are necessary.

The Essence of Visionary Leadership

Visionary leadership involves setting a clear direction for the brand and inspiring others to follow. It requires foresight, creativity, and the ability to communicate a compelling vision that aligns with the brand's long-term goals. Effective leaders in the fashion industry are adept at navigating the market's complexities, fostering innovation, and driving change.

As we have studied and attended different training sessions in our organisations, there are various leadership styles. Leadership styles can significantly impact team dynamics, productivity, and overall organisational success.

Building a Strong Team

A strong team is the backbone of any successful fashion brand. Recruiting individuals who share the brand's vision and values is crucial. However, building a team goes beyond hiring the right people; it involves creating an environment where employees feel valued, motivated, and empowered to contribute their best work.

- Companies like Lululemon prioritise cultural fit during recruitment to ensure that new hires align with the brand's values and ethos.
- Providing opportunities for professional growth and development is essential for retaining top talent.
- Patagonia offers extensive training programmes and career development opportunities to help employees advance within the company.
- Encouraging collaboration and fostering a sense of community within the team can lead to higher productivity and innovation.

- ◦ Warby Parker emphasises teamwork and collaboration, with initiatives that bring employees together across different departments.

Fostering a Positive Culture

A positive organisational culture is key to employee satisfaction and brand loyalty. It encompasses the values, beliefs, and behaviours that define how employees interact and work together. Leaders play a critical role in shaping and maintaining this culture.

How to Build a Positive Culture

1. **Open Communication**:
   - ◦ Creating an environment where employees feel comfortable sharing ideas and feedback.
2. **Recognition and Reward**:
   - ◦ Acknowledging and rewarding employees' contributions fosters a sense of appreciation and motivation.
3. **Work-Life Balance**:
   - ◦ Promoting work-life balance is crucial for employee well-being and productivity.

I want to emphasise the summary of the key concepts related to leadership and vision from Jim Collins' book **"good to great"**: The concepts have been enumerated in his book with extensive research, and it helps new executives to build great organisations.

The key takeaways are as follows.

1. Level 5 Leaders: Level 5 Leadership

- A unique blend of personal humility and professorship. These leaders are ambitious for the company's success, not their own, and they prepare their successors for outstanding achievements.

- **Key Traits**: Level 5 leaders display compelling modesty, self-effacing behaviour, and an unwavering resolve to produce sustained results. They take full responsibility for failures and attribute successes to external factors.

The author has provided examples of great companies like Kimberly-Clark, Fannie Mae, Gillette, and Abbott Laboratories.

2. First Who, Then What

- Good to great companies prioritise hiring the right people before deciding on a direction or strategy. This involves rigorous selection to hire only those who fit the company's culture and future vision.
- The right people create the right culture, which drives the right results.

3. Confronting the Brutal Facts

- Successful companies face the reality of their situation, no matter how harsh it might be. They create an environment where the truth is heard and acted upon without hierarchy or charisma deterring it. Engage in dialogue and debate, not coercion.
- Build a red flag mechanism.
- Facing the brutal facts allows companies to make necessary adjustments and sustain growth.

4. The Hedgehog Concept

- The Hedgehog Concept of focusing on what you can be the best at, driven by passion and a clear economic driver. This simple yet profound focus allows companies to transcend competence and achieve greatness.

- It involves understanding what you are passionate about, what you can be the best at, and what drives your economic engine.

5. Culture of Discipline

- A disciplined culture, where self-motivated individuals follow a consistent system, is key to sustained success. This approach avoids the pitfalls of bureaucracy and stifles creativity and innovation.
- Discipline ensures that the right people are doing the right things correctly.

6. The Flywheel and the Doom Loop

- The journey from good to great is a cumulative process, not a sudden transformation. It takes consistent effort over time to build momentum, leading to breakthroughs.
- Companies that try to achieve quick fixes end up in a doom loop, lurching from one quick fix to another without maintaining a consistent direction.

7. Good is the Enemy of Great

- Many companies never become great because they become too good and settle for mediocrity. Greatness requires a conscious choice to pursue excellence and continuous improvement.

By focusing on these principles, companies can transform from good to great, achieving sustained excellence and outperforming their competitors.

Leading with vision in the fashion industry involves more than managing day-to-day operations. It requires a holistic approach that prioritises team building, fosters a positive culture, and aligns with the brand's goals. By embracing these principles, fashion leaders can create a thriving work environment that drives innovation, enhances employee satisfaction, and propels the brand to new heights.

Key Takeaways from Chapter Building a Strong Team and Culture:

Fashion Leadership Beyond the Office

Adapting to New Generation Employees

- **Digital Integration:** Utilise advanced digital tools for communication, collaboration, and project management.
- **Continuous Learning:** Provide opportunities for upskilling and reskilling through online courses, workshops, and mentorship.
- **Collaborative Environment:** Foster a culture that values diversity, inclusion, and open communication.
- **Work-Life Balance:** Offer flexible work arrangements, including remote work options and flexible hours.
- **Meaningful Work:** Emphasise sustainability, ethical practices, and social responsibility to attract and retain employees.
- **Recognition and Rewards:** Implement programmes to recognise and reward employee contributions.
- **Employee Well-Being:** Prioritise wellness programmes, mental health support, and a healthy work environment.

Visionary Leadership

- **Clear Direction:** Set a compelling vision that aligns with the brand's long-term goals.
- **Inspire and Navigate:** Foster innovation, drive change, and navigate market complexities.
- **Leadership Styles:** Adapt leadership styles to influence team dynamics, productivity, and organisational success.

Building a Strong Team

- **Cultural Fit:** Recruit individuals who align with the brand's vision and values.
- **Professional Growth:** Provide training programmes and career development opportunities.
- **Collaboration:** Encourage teamwork and foster a sense of community.

Fostering a Positive Culture

- **Open Communication:** Create an environment for sharing ideas and feedback.
- **Recognition and Reward:** Acknowledge and reward contributions to foster appreciation and motivation.
- **Work-Life Balance:** Promote practices that ensure employee well-being and productivity.

Leadership Insights from "good to great" by Jim Collins

1. **Level 5 Leadership:** Blend personal humility and professional will; ambitious for the company, not personal success.
2. **First Who, Then What:** Prioritise hiring the right people before setting direction or strategy.
3. **Confronting the Brutal Facts:** Face harsh realities and create an environment where the truth is heard.
4. **The Hedgehog Concept:** Focus on what you can be the best at, driven by passion and a clear economic driver.
5. **Culture of Discipline:** Maintain a disciplined culture where self-motivated individuals follow a consistent system.
6. **The Flywheel and the Doom Loop:** Build momentum gradually through consistent effort, avoiding quick fixes.
7. **Good is the Enemy of Great:** Pursue excellence and continuous improvement, avoiding complacency.

Leading with vision in the fashion industry involves more than managing daily operations. It requires building a strong team, fostering a positive culture, and aligning with the brand's goals. By embracing these principles and adapting to the needs of new generation employees, fashion leaders can create a thriving work environment that drives innovation, enhances employee satisfaction, and propels the brand to new heights.

Conclusion

This book provides a roadmap for entrepreneurs looking to build a fashion brand that lasts by focusing on foundational principles, product development, and scaling strategies. The chapters emphasise the importance of aligning your brand's purpose with sustainability, quality, and emotional storytelling, while using agile methods to test and validate ideas before scaling.

Part 1: Nurturing the Idea

Chapter 1: Beyond Trends - Building Timeless Value

- **Key Takeaway:** Fashion brands must transcend fleeting trends to build lasting value, focusing on authenticity and purpose-driven values.
- **Actionable Insights**
  - Develop a brand rooted in sustainability, inclusivity, or cultural preservation.
  - Prioritise quality over quantity, using premium materials and artisan craftsmanship, such as in Hermès products.
  - Align your brand with cultural or historical relevance to create a deeper connection with your audience.

Chapter 2: From Why to Vision

- **Key Takeaway:** A brand's "why" drives its vision and purpose, and this clarity helps the brand differentiate itself in a crowded market.
- **Actionable Insights:**
    - Articulate your brand's purpose beyond profit. Align it with values like sustainability or inclusivity.
    - Use the **Golden Circle Framework** (Why, How, What) to structure your messaging.
    - Regularly revisit your brand's purpose to ensure it stays true to its core values while adapting to market needs.

Chapter 3: From Idea to MVP – Building the Foundation

- **Key Takeaway:** Start with a Minimum Viable Product (MVP) to test and validate ideas quickly, ensuring cost-effectiveness and faster market entry.
- **Actionable Insights**
    - Focus on solving the core problem with a simplified version of your product.
    - Use feedback loops like **Build-Measure-Learn** to refine the product.
    - Keep the MVP lean, avoiding over-engineering, and use tools like the **Business Model Canvas** (BMC) to plan effectively.
    - Leverage customer feedback from surveys, pre-orders, and small product launches to fine-tune the product.

Chapter 4: "Threads of Connection: Crafting a Brand Story That Resonates"

- **Key Takeaway:** A compelling brand story is essential for differentiating your brand and building emotional connections with your audience.

- **Actionable Insights**
  - Share your origin story, challenges, and how your brand aligns with customer values.
  - Ensure consistency in your narrative across all touchpoints, from social media to product packaging.
  - Build emotional connections by telling stories that evoke joy, nostalgia, or hope.
  - Focus on authenticity and relatability to foster trust and loyalty.

Part 2: Product and Launch – Key Takeaways

The Power of Product Positioning

Product positioning is crucial for creating a distinct brand identity that emotionally connects with consumers. Differentiation helps brands stand out in a crowded market, answering critical questions such as: *What makes your brand unique?* and *What emotional need does it address?*

Best Practices for Differentiation in Apparel

- **Value-Based Differentiation:** Align your brand with values like sustainability, as seen with Patagonia.
- **Niche Focus:** Cater to specific market segments for strong loyalty (e.g., Decathlon's sports-specific focus).
- **Quality and Craftsmanship:** Emphasise superior materials and production techniques (e.g., Levi's durable denim).
- **Innovative Design:** Introduce new functionality or aesthetics (e.g. Uniqlo's HeatTech fabric).

Customer-Centric Approach

- Understand and prioritise customer needs through research and feedback.
- Personalise experiences to build trust and relevance.

Importance of Sustainable Product Design

- Sustainable design practices reduce environmental and social impacts, which are becoming a competitive advantage. Brands like Patagonia and Adidas integrate sustainability with innovation.

Material Innovation

- Emerging materials like organic cotton, mushroom leather, and biodegradable plastics promote resource conservation.
- Bio-based innovations from companies like TomTex (using shrimp shells) offer plastic-free, biodegradable options.

Circular Design Principles

- Design products for longevity, repairability, and recyclability. Circular models (e.g., rental, resale, repair) help decouple growth from resource consumption.

Transparency and Traceability

- Share supply chain data through blockchain and certifications like Fair Trade to build consumer trust.

Trend and Competitor Analysis

Trend and competitor analysis helps anticipate market demands and refine value propositions. These analyses provide valuable insights into consumer behaviour, market gaps, and industry shifts.

Key Frameworks for Competitor Analysis

- **Strategic Group Analysis:** Group competitors by factors like pricing or market share.
- **SWOT Analysis:** Evaluate strengths, weaknesses, opportunities, and threats.
- **Porter's Five Forces:** Assess competition, buyer/supplier power, and market barriers.

Fashion Trend Forecasting

- Predicting trends involves cultural, economic, and technological influences. Agencies like WGSN and Heuritech use AI and social media to offer actionable insights.

The Central Role of the Product Manager

Fashion product managers are integral to the brand's success, acting as orchestrators between research, design, sourcing, production, marketing, and sales.

Responsibilities of a Product Manager

- **Product Development:** Ensure products align with market needs and brand identity.
- **Market Research:** Stay ahead of trends and consumer preferences.
- **Go-to-Market Strategy:** Plan a robust product launch and promotional efforts.

Product Development Process

From ideation to post-launch analysis, product managers oversee the entire lifecycle, using tools like tech packs and PLM software to streamline production.

Leveraging Tools and Strategies

- Platforms like PLM software and project management tools (e.g. Asana) increase team productivity and efficiency.

Laying Down Brand Launch Guidelines (Go-to-Market Plan)

A solid Go-to-Market (GTM) plan is key for positioning your brand, reaching the target audience, and ensuring a successful launch.

Market Research and Analysis

- Conduct surveys and competitive analysis to define your target audience and brand positioning.

Product and Inventory Management

- Ensure products are quality-checked and inventory is properly planned to avoid shortages or excess stock.

Effective Marketing and Promotion

- Build a strong digital presence and leverage influencer partnerships.
- Create engaging content to attract and retain your audience.

Launch Channels and Strategies

- Utilise e-commerce and physical retail (e.g. pop-up shops) for flexibility and reach.

Building Pre-Launch Hype

- Use teaser campaigns, influencer collaborations, and exclusive events to generate excitement before the launch.

Public Relations and Press Coverage

- Secure media coverage and collaborate with fashion journalists to amplify your brand's unique story.

Monitoring and Adaptability

- Track metrics like website traffic, social media engagement, and sales to adjust strategies dynamically.

By following these guidelines, leveraging strategic planning, and focusing on sustainable design, material innovation, and market differentiation, fashion brands can achieve successful launches and long-term growth.

Part 3: Scaling

The Art of Sourcing and Inventory Management

1. **Sourcing as a Strategic Pillar**

   Effective sourcing isn't just about operational efficiency—it builds a brand's identity and differentiates it in the market. Brands like Patagonia have demonstrated the power of aligning sourcing practices with sustainability.

2. **The Critical Role of Speed and Adaptability**

   Agility in sourcing allows brands to quickly adapt to fast-changing trends. Companies like Zara exemplify how agile supply chains can minimise waste and respond to market demands.

3. **Agile Design and Supply Chain Streamlining**

   Agile methodologies help reduce product development cycles and create more responsive supply chains. Using ERP systems, local sourcing, and lean manufacturing enables greater cost efficiency.

4. **Technological Integration in Inventory Management**

   Advances like AI, blockchain, and IoT are revolutionising inventory management, improving accuracy, reducing waste, and increasing transparency.

5. **Sustainability in Sourcing and Inventory Management**

   Sustainable sourcing is essential, aligning with consumer expectations and regulatory pressures. Brands such as Patagonia's Worn Wear programme exemplify how sustainability can reduce costs and build brand loyalty.

6. **Data-Driven Decision Making**

   AI and real-time data integration help forecast demand, optimise stock levels, and improve supply chain performance, driving efficiency.

7. **Technological Innovations in Inventory Management**

   Technologies like RFID, AI, and cloud-based systems improve efficiency, accuracy, and reduce operational costs in inventory management.

Key Takeaways from Scaling Your Brand:

1. **Strategic Scaling**

   Scaling involves more than increasing production—it requires operational efficiency, market expansion, and technology integration to ensure long-term sustainability and growth.

2. **Market Expansion**

   Expansion into new markets, both domestically and internationally, requires understanding local consumer behaviours and preferences.

3. **Product Diversification**

   Offering a variety of products or collaborating with other brands can mitigate risks and attract a broader customer base.

4. **Leveraging Technology**

   Utilising advanced technologies for data analytics, personalised marketing, and inventory management helps scale operations efficiently.

5. **Comprehensive Planning**

   Scaling requires strategic planning, including assessing operational readiness, market demand, and competitive landscape. Operational efficiency and cash flow management are key considerations.

Key Takeaways from Product Line Expansion:

1. **Strategic Approach**

   Expanding your product line should be strategic, introducing complementary products that align with your brand's identity and consumer needs.

2. **Market Research & Competitive Analysis**

   Understanding gaps in the market and consumer preferences helps identify the right opportunities for product line expansion.

3. **Enhancing Operational Efficiency**

   Automation, lean manufacturing, and optimised supply chains are critical for managing the increased complexity of a broader product line.

4. **Leveraging Data and Analytics**

   Data can be used to inform decisions about customer insights, demand forecasting, and inventory management to ensure a successful product expansion.

Key Takeaways from Building a Strong Brand Community:

1. **Importance of a Brand Community**

   A strong brand community builds loyalty, provides valuable feedback, and fosters positive word-of-mouth marketing.

2. **Engaging Content and Social Media**

   Authentic storytelling and active engagement on social media are vital for building connections with your audience.

3. **Loyalty Programmes and Rewards:**

   Rewarding loyal customers with incentives such as exclusive offers and early access enhances engagement and retention.

Key Takeaways from Measuring Success and Adjusting Strategies:

1. **Data-Driven Decisions**

   Tracking key metrics such as revenue growth, customer acquisition cost, and customer lifetime value ensures that strategies are optimised and aligned with business objectives.

2. **Adjusting Strategies**

   Continuously analysing trends and customer feedback allows brands to adjust their strategies to improve marketing, sales, and customer engagement.

Key Takeaways from Building a Strong Team and Culture:

1. **Visionary Leadership**

   Leaders in fashion must set a clear direction, inspire teams, and navigate challenges while aligning with the company's long-term goals.

2. **Building a Strong Team**

   Hiring people who align with your brand's values and fostering a collaborative environment helps cultivate a strong, innovative team.

3. **Fostering a Positive Culture**

   Emphasising open communication, employee well-being, and work-life balance attracts and retains top talent.

4. **Leadership Insights**

   Principles from "good to great" guide leaders to create a disciplined, innovative, and effective work culture focused on long-term success.

Acknowledgements

My sincere acknowledgements to the people who came in my professional life and made a difference in the growth of my career.

1. Mr. Anindya Ray – Co-Founder BlueKaktus I Founder & CEO Studio-Earth
2. Mr. Samrat Som – Brand Design Strategy Consultant
3. Mr. Vasuki K R – Behavioural trainer & Textile & Apparel technical Product trainer
4. Mr. Prabhakar Babu Rao – Manager sourcing & Merchandising
5. Mr. Anand Aiyer – Chief Executive Officer - Arrow I Arvind Brands
6. Mr. Puneet Sood – Global Head – Brand Operations, CX & Strategic Projects at Royal Enfeild
7. Mr. Anand John Joseph – Head – Corporate HR | Business Anticipator, People leader with a Socio-Entrepreneurial mindset
8. Mr. Anurag Kapur – Format Sourcing Head : Azorte
9. Mr. Jacob John – President at Aditya Birla Fashion and Retail Ltd
10. Mohit Bhasin – Dept. General Manager, Redington
11. Siddhartha Lal – Exec. Chairman, Eicher Motors Ltd
12. B. Govindarajan – MD EML and CEO of Royal Enfield

All the Gurus, Well-wishers, friends who has helped me gain the knowledge in the industry.

Notes: Illustration Credits

Global Apparel Market Statistics & Facts

https://www.statista.com/topics/5091/apparel-market-worldwide/#topicOverview

Brand value of the top ten apparel brands worldwide in 2024 (in a million U.S. dollars)

https://www.statista.com/statistics/267931/brand-value-of-the-leading-10-apparel-brands-worldwide/

Fashion Industry Trends & Outlook for 2024-25: Navigating a Challenging Era. Vishakha Somani, Assistant Manager, is a Fashion Tech Analyst and Communications expert at WFX - World Fashion Exchange.

https://www.worldfashionexchange.com/blog/fashion-trends-2024-25/

Chapter 1

1—**Patagonia's Website & Environmental Activism Pages**: Patagonia's official site includes information on the *"Don't Buy This Jacket"* campaign, the Worn Wear programme, and its environmental commitments. It provides detailed explanations of the philosophy behind these initiatives and how they align with the brand's mission.

- Website: www.patagonia.com

Yvon Chouinard's Book - *Let My People Go Surfing*: In this book, Chouinard discusses Patagonia's environmental values, the company's mission, and details on various campaigns, including *"Don't Buy This Jacket."* It provides insights into the brand's ethical stance on consumption and environmental responsibility.

Harvard Business Review and Case Studies on Patagonia: Articles from HBR and other business publications frequently use Patagonia as a case study for sustainable and purpose-driven branding. One notable HBR article, *"Patagonia's Anti-Growth Strategy,"* explores the impact of the *"Don't Buy This Jacket"* campaign on consumer behaviour and the company's reputation.

- Article link: Harvard Business Review

The New York Times, *The Guardian*, and Forbes: Major news outlets have reported on Patagonia's campaigns and the ethos behind their anti-consumerist message. They often cover the broader cultural and environmental impact of Patagonia's campaigns.

- For example, a *New York Times* article titled *"Patagonia to Politicians: Keep Your Climate Promises or Keep Your Fleeces"* explores Patagonia's advocacy-driven campaigns.

This is the key to breakthrough innovation, according to a 3M scientist - Forbes.com

Chapter 3

Teaching MBAs How to Design: Experimenting at the Haas School of Business Sara L. Beckman, Clark Kellogg, and Helene Cahen

https://faculty.haas.berkeley.edu/lyons/BeckmanDesign.pdf

Business Model Canvas Explained: Definition and Components

Written by MasterClass

Last updated: 22nd September 2021

https://www.masterclass.com/articles/business-model-canvas-explained#4h2VBxirdmiFgs82eMtFVC

15 Ethnographic Interview Questions with Examples

Bella Williams

https://insight7.io/15-ethnographic-interview-questions-with-examples/

63% of consumers prefer to purchase from purpose-driven brands, study finds

https://www.marketingdive.com/news/63-of-consumers-prefer-to-purchase-from-purpose-driven-brands-study-finds/543712/

The State of Fashion 2024: Finding pockets of growth as uncertainty reigns

https://www.mckinsey.com/industries/retail/our-insights/state-of-fashion-2024#

The State of Fashion 2025

https://www.mckinsey.com/~/media/mckinsey/industries/retail/our%20insights/state%20of%20fashion/2025/the-state-of-fashion-2025-v2.pdf?shouldIndex=false

Experience is everything; here's how to get it right.

https://www.pwc.de/de/consulting/pwc-consumer-intelligence-series-customer-experience.pdf?utm_source=chatgpt.com

Chapter 4

The rules of international business are being rewritten, creating opportunities for companies that are nimble enough to capitalise. BCG's international business consultants help companies recognise the economic patterns in globalisation and seize the future.

Retail Industry, Consumer Products Industry, International Business

How Innovation and Collaboration Can Accelerate Sustainability in Fashion - July 14, 2017

https://www.bcg.com/publications/2017/retail-how-innovation-collaboration-accelerate-sustainability-fashion

Sustainable style: How fashion can afford and accelerate decarbonisation

28th March 2024 | Article

https://www.mckinsey.com/industries/retail/our-insights/sustainable-style-how-fashion-can-afford-and-accelerate-decarbonization

Sustainable style: How fashion can afford and accelerate decarbonisation. Translating fashion's decarbonisation commitments into action has proved difficult. A new McKinsey analysis outlines what the industry can do to reach its targets.

- by Jonatan Janmark, Karl-Hendrik Magnus, Ignacio Marcos, and Evan Wiener

https://www.mckinsey.com/~/media/mckinsey/industries/retail/our%20insights/sustainable%20style%20how%20fashion%20can%20afford%20and%20accelerate%20decarbonization/sustainablestyle-how-fashion-can-afford-and-accelerate-decarbonization-final.pdf?shouldIndex=false

For more insights into sustainable practices in the apparel industry, visit resources like Boston Consulting Group's sustainability analysis and MDPI's studies on fashion innovation.

The Most Exciting Advancements in Fabric Innovation Right Now - Fashionista

These are the New Sustainable Materials in Fashion in 2024

Fashion and a Circular Economy | Ellen MacArthur Foundation

Weekday

Cross Textiles

15 More Sustainable Fashion Brands Leading the Circular Economy - Good On You

Competitive Environment Analysis: The 3 Frameworks.

Maven: 9 Types of Competitor Analysis Frameworks to Master

Fashion Trend Forecasting: How Brands Predict New Styles - 2023 - EpiProdux Blog

Introducing a revolutionary new plant root textile

https://www.rootfull.com/fashion

Chapter 6

https://venngage.com/blog/branding-statistics/

The Power of Brand Authenticity on Social Media [Infographic]

Authenticity can inspire trust and loyalty - and drive ROI. By Kimberlee Morrison April 6, 2015

Chapter 8

The role of inventory management in sustainability and ethical sourcing

https://elmasys.com/blog/the-role-of-inventory-management-in-sustainability-and-ethical-sourcing/

Official Sustainable Fashion Statistics

https://theroundup.org/sustainable-fashion-statistics/

Chapter 9

Exploring the Ins and Outs of Product Development in Fashion: From Sketch to Sample

By rHappy Sharer

Jun 16, 2023 Creative Skills, Fashion Industry, Marketing Campaigns, Product Development, Technical Skills

https://www.researchgate.net/publication/383209212_Analyzing_the_Impact_of_Marketing_Strategy_A_Case_Study_of_Nike_Air_Max_1/fulltext/66c2019c8d007355925fd137/Analyzing-the-Impact-of-Marketing-Strategy-A-Case-Study-of-Nike-Air-Max-1.pdf

Nike Global Marketing Strategy 2024: A Case Study

By Nina Sheridan

https://www.latterly.org/nike-global-marketing-strategy/

Chapter 10

Good to Great by Jim Collins – Book Summary and Notes

https://www.justologist.com/good-to-great/

Developing the New Generation of Workers

Barbara Osiecka

https://wowledge.com/blog/developing-the-new-generation-of-workers

The Millennials: A new generation of employees, a new set of engagement policies

by: Jay Gilbert

https://iveybusinessjournal.com/publication/the-millennials-a-new-generation-of-employees-a-new-set-of-engagement-policies/

Building Workforce Resilience in the Fashion and Luxury Goods Industry

https://www.aon.com/en/insights/articles/building-workforce-resilience-in-the-fashion-and-luxury-goods-industry

About the Author

Prashanta HV is an alumnus of Haas School of Business, UC Berkeley, a seasoned expert in product strategy, sourcing, buying, and merchandising with over two decades of experience in the fashion and apparel industry. As a visionary leader, Prasshant has made a significant impact on some of the most recognisable brands in India, showcasing his ability to build, transform, and scale businesses to new heights. His work is deeply rooted in innovation, sustainability, and a relentless drive to deliver value to customers and stakeholders.

Prasshant's career spans prestigious organisations such as Royal Enfield Apparel, Arvind Lifestyle Brands, Aditya Birla Lifestyle Brands, and Himatsingka Seide Ltd., where he has played pivotal roles in brand building, product development, and supply chain optimisation. At Royal Enfield Apparel, Prasshant led the business through remarkable growth, taking it from inception to a multiple X revenue increase in just nine years. He redefined product portfolios, streamlined operations, and introduced groundbreaking sustainable products, including the first-ever completely sustainable riding jackets in the industry.

With a strong belief in aligning purpose with innovation, Prasshant has spearheaded collaborations with globally renowned brands. His leadership has been instrumental in launching industry-first initiatives, like CE-certified riding jackets in India and eco-friendly packaging solutions, setting new benchmarks for sustainability in the apparel sector.

Prasshant's academic credentials are equally impressive. He holds a Bachelor of Technology in Textile Technology and a Postgraduate Diploma in Marketing Management. Further enhancing his expertise, he completed the prestigious Executive Programme in Management at the Haas School of Business, UC Berkeley, earning a Certificate of Business Excellence.

His achievements include developing innovative products like the "SuperLuxe" stitchless shirt for Arrow. Prasshant's work reflects his deep commitment to creating products that combine functionality, aesthetics, and sustainability, empowering brands to stand out in competitive markets.

Beyond his professional accomplishments, Prasshant is a passionate advocate for continuous learning, mentorship, and building a culture of excellence. His journey is an inspiring testament to the power of strategic thinking, creative problem-solving, and unwavering dedication to excellence.

In this book, Prasshant distils years of experience into actionable insights, providing readers with a comprehensive roadmap to navigate and thrive in the ever-evolving world of fashion. Whether you're an aspiring entrepreneur, a seasoned professional, or a student with big dreams, Prasshant's wisdom and expertise will guide you towards building a successful and impactful brand.

www.ingramcontent.com/pod-product-compliance
Ingram Content Group UK Ltd.
Pitfield, Milton Keynes, MK11 3LW, UK
UKHW041634190726
13854UKWH00006B/2495

9 798896 737650